Preface

Late in 1977, Expertise International completed a multiclient study on distributed processing. The study encompassed in-depth discussions throughout the U.S.A. and Europe with many managers of installed distributed systems, manufacturers, consultants, system and software houses along with research on the current relevant literature. The initial report was published as four volumes:

> Management Report
> Technical Report
> Installation Reports
> Supplementary Papers

Subsequently, Q.E.D. Information Sciences, Inc. reviewed the report, restructured it into its current volumes:

> Management Report - Volume I
> Technical Report - Volume II

This Management Report contains the findings of the study written for management readers who are acquainted with the basic concepts and terminology of data processing. The motivations for distributed processing are explored and the practicalities of the technique documented in some detail. Because of the influence of IBM in the market place (and because many of our project sponsors are IBM users), a special section on IBM's approach to distributed data processing is included. Other sections consider future trends, financial issues and implications of distributed processing for management and the data processing department. The report concludes with management guidelines for the planning of distributed systems. In addition, included are three supplemental papers that we felt would provide additional viewpoints. These papers are also included in the Technical Report.

As in any study of this nature, the assistance, cooperation and participation of many knowledgeable and talented people is required. We would like to thank them. They are listed in no particular order. Our apologies to anyone who has been inadvertently overlooked.

Phil Dorn, Dorn Computer Consultants, New York.
Frank Benevento, Citibank, New York.
David Williams, IBM, White Plains, New York.
Bob Coales, IBM United Kingdom, London.
Jim MacDonald, Pacific Stereo, San Francisco.
Chuck Montequin, Converse Rubber, Wilmington, Mass.
Jack Jones, Southern Railway System, Atlanta, Georgia.
Andy Copanas (and colleagues), DEC, Maynard, Mass.
Barry Jones, DEC, UK.
Jim Butts, Bank of America, San Francisco.
Martin Toomey, Four-Phase Systems, Cupertino, California

Jack Faulhaber, Gulf Atlantic Distribution Services, Houston, Texas.
Rusty Gordon, IST Datasystems, Memphis, Tenn.
Louis Pouzin, IRIA, France.
Barry Spatz (and colleagues), IBM, Boca Raton, Florida.
Frank Taylor, NCC, Manchester, England.
Roger Green, NCC, Manachester, England.
Alan Horner, MODCOMP, Ft. Lauderdale, Florida.
Jan Jagerstrom, Minfo Konsultgrupp AB, Gothenberg, Sweden.
Martin Healey, University College, Cardiff.
Jeremy Salter (and colleagues), Norsk Data, Oslo, Norway.
John Jennings, Tilling Management Services Ltd., London.
Mike Brunton, Makro, Manchester, England.
John Beecher, W.R. Grace, London.
Alan Scarisbrick, IBM, United Kingdom.
Ben Bevis, Fireman's Fund, San Raphael, California.
Robert Cook, J.C. Penney Co., New York.
Art Esch, Decision Strategy Corporation, New York.
Jim Oyler, Harris Data Systems, Dallas, Texas.
Mike Tucker, Harris Data Systems, UK.
Alan Watson, Ventek, London.
David Baker, Datapoint, San Antionio, Texas.
Mike Schwartz, Quaker City Motor Parts, Middletown, Delware.
Saroj Kar, TCT International, Sunnyvale, California.
Paul Lindfors, IBM, Research Triangle Park, N.C.
Jim Gray, IBM, Research Triangle Park, N.C.
Gary Schmidt, IBM, Research Triangle Park, N.C.
Donald Alusic, DEC, Maynard, Mass.
Sam Marzullo, Texas Instruments, Houston.
James Booth, Motorola, Scottsdale, Arizona.

Expertise International
1978

Distributed Processing:

Current practice and future developments

Vol. 1: Management Report

An Expertise International
Multiclient Report

Q.E.D. Information Sciences, Inc.
Wellesley, Massachusetts 02181

Printed in the United States of America by
Q.E.D. Information Sciences, Inc.
141 Linden Street
Wellesley, MA 02181

Contents

References are made in this report to Supplementary Papers (SP) and
Installation Reports (IR) which are contained in Volume 2 of this series.
These reports provide more detailed and in-depth reviews of many of the
subjects discussed in this management report.

GLOSSARY OF ABBREVIATIONS

Because of the extensive use of mnemonics throughout this report, we felt it would aid the readability if we included this brief glossary.

ACF   –   Advanced Communications Adapter
ARM   –   Asynchronous Response Mode
BAD   –   Bisynchronous Assembler/Dissassembler
BSC   –   Binary Synchronous Communication
BSI   –   British Standards Institute
DAP   –   Data Access Protocol
DCE   –   Data Communication Equipment
DDP   –   Distributed Data Processing
DDCMP –   Digital Data Communications Message Protocol
DNA   –   Distributed Network Architecture – National Cash Register
DTE   –   Data Terminal Equipment
FAD   –   Frame Assembler/Disassembler
FCX   –   Frame Check Sequence
FDX   –   Full Duplex Transmission
FEP   –   Front End Processor
HDLC –   High Level Data Link Control
HLP   –   High Level Protocol
HDX   –   Half Duplex Transmission
ICA   –   Intergrated Communication Adaptor
ISO   –   International Standards Organization
LAP   –   Link Access Protocol
NRM   –   Normal Response Mode
NSP   –   Network Services Protocol
PDN   –   Public Data Networks
PAD   –   Packet Assembler/Disassembler
PSTN –   Public Switched Telephone Network
PTT   –   Post Telegraph and Telephone Public Telephone Companies
SBCS –   Small Business Computers
SNA   –   System Network Architecture – IBM
SPC   –   Stored Program Control
VDU   –   Visual Display Unit

CHAPTER 1

A MANAGEMENT PERSPECTIVE

"Distributed Data Processing is a fad..."
                                                    Gene Amdahl

*"DDP reflects the freeing of computer users from
 the grasps of technology..."*
                                                    IDC Report

1.1 INTRODUCTION

An interesting disparity of views. Only ten years ago, similar stances were being taken with respect to the use of terminals as an extension of centralized data processing operations.

In this section of the Management Report on Distributed Systems, we shall attempt to put the technique in the context of historical trends in data processing.   We shall also identify the various influences which have stimulated both interest and activity in this area. The astute reader will have noticed that we have managed to reach well into the second paragraph of the report without attempting to define "distributed processing". If all goes well, definitions shall be left to Chapter 2 where we can get down to practicalities.

1.2 SOME HISTORY

Many of you have been in data processing long enough to remember the installation of single batch-processing business computers for single-application projects. Such computers were relatively simple; files were mainly held on magnetic tape and the use of disk was limited. There were no operating systems and highlevel languages and single programs were run at a time. The management approach was similarly unsophisticated; an area of need was identified and a computer acquired to meet that need (Figure 1). As other possibilities were identified, it was generally necessary to buy another computer; even if the existing one could be expanded in size the relatively crude software did not permit any great degree of overlapped processing.

For many corporations, this led to the "1401 on every floor" syndrome whereby each department, division or subsidiary had its own small system. This trend was encountered in the early 1960's, with the announcement by IBM of the System/360 with its multipurpose, multiprogramming Operating System. Unlike the earlier technology, the 360 was a range of machines and this has been significant in the growth of the centralized dp facility. It was not difficult for IBM to demonstrate clear economies of scale. Grosch's Law was born and operations to tidy-up data processing activities were initiated.

The improved control software which grew up to parallel the 360 (and similar processors from other suppliers) enabled the extra power to be utilized efficiently in a multiprogramming batch environment. Files became more sophisticated and we saw greater use of direct access storage in

Figure 1

Trends in Corporate Data Processing

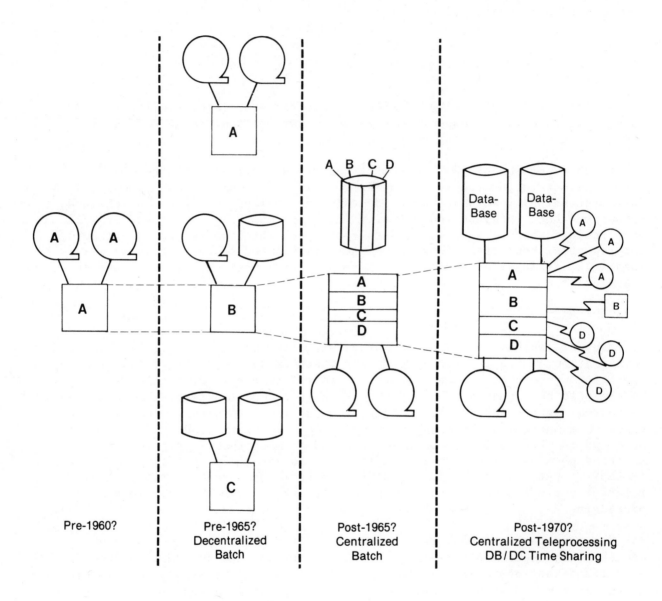

preference to tape (but without replacing it). Early database systems were tried with variable success. As the power of the central facility increased, so did the power of dp management and the importance of its role within the organization.

Few people would argue that, although this approach could achieve well-defined economies, service to the user department (and, in turn, to their users or customers) was often impaired. This problem arose because, although we were automating the data processing and data storage aspect of corporate activities, data communications was not automated at all. The use of mail and messenger to transport data between user departments and the dp facility made the effect of centralization acutely felt by the remote sites. In addition, such a heavy commitment by line departments on a service department for fundamental day-to-day support was arguably an unhealthy situation for both parties.

Attempts to overcome this problem lead us to the next phase of organizational dp use. The installation of remote batch terminals provided the user department with easier means of access to the central facility without any fundamental changes to application program and methods of working.

Given a choice, an increasing number of new applications were implemented using interactive terminals (such as visual displays). This trend ought to have had a significant impact on the way in which we use computers. Indeed, in many companies it has; service to line departments improved and the ability to work interactively with the computer increased levels of job satisfaction.

However, centralized "teleprocessing" has for many organizations been less than satisfactory. The reasons for this are both management and technical. Too often, the interactive approach was viewed as a means of "patching up" the problems of a batch system. For example, it is still not uncommon to hear that a major reason for installing terminals was to "improve customer service". Further study often shows that the only reason why customer service needs improving is because it deteriorated when the centralized batch system was installed. In other words, new technological investments were being made to solve problems caused by earlier technological investments; we had lost sight of corporate objectives.

The technical reasons for the failure of teleprocessing systems are based upon a lack of awareness of the differences between this approach and batch processing. It has been in the interest of computer suppliers to over-simplify the differences and, consequently, dp management has under-invested in the acquisition of new skills in preparation for the design and development of online systems. The results of this have been poor response times, lack of program maintainability, ill-considered user/terminal dialogues, inadequate failsafety and limited expansion capability. In the author's opinion, the hardware and software approach to data communications by most mainframe suppliers has caused teleprocessing to be viewed as an expensive concept. This is unfair; as we shall see later, the minicomputer has shown how inexpensive online operations can be.

In this same phase of dp developments we have also seen increased interest in the use of database technology. The centralizing of data goes hand in hand with the centralizing of processing. The potential benefits of database managements (DBMS) are well understood; reduced redundacy, data independence for programs and so on. The problem with DBMS is that, arguably, the concept is well in advance of current direct access storage technology. In the past 20 years, almost all R & D has gone into improving recording densities. Relatively, access times have hardly improved at all over the same period. Until there is a significant breakthrough in the technology of mass direct access storage, then it is hard to see how much can be done to improve the present, generally inadequate, performance of DBMS. It is rapidly becoming accepted that the only way to administer databases in a timely and accurate manner is through terminals. The response-time needs of such interactive terminals serves to highlight to the end-user the performance problems just described.

So that is where we are at the moment; online databases (DB/DC in IBM terminology), remote batch, transaction processing and perhaps some interactive program development or a time-sharing service for technical departments.

1.3 PRESSURES TO DECENTRALIZE

In spite of the relative sophistication and cost of many of today's computer systems, it would be unrealistic to suppose that everybody is happy. User dissatisfaction has long been recognized. During the course of this study, it became clear that there is increasing disillusionment with the centralized "mainframe" approach on the part of dp managers and their technical staff. It seems to be difficult to resist an almost indomitable trend to larger and more complex central site configurations. In spite of virtual storage and cheaper main memory, installations are spending more and more on main memory (regardless of application needs). Although processors tend to be very reliable, management is nervous about committing so many critical applications to a single machine.

It is by no means unusual for more than 60% of staff budgets to be allocated to the maintenance of existing applications. Certainly in Europe, personnel with the right skills and experience seem to be ever more difficult to find.

From the user's point of view he is often seeing a monolithic, remote and overburdened dp department which is not only out of touch with his needs but does not even have the time to look at them. Requests for system changes and improvements get dealt with eventually, but new applications may have to wait for years. It is easy to understand why the user of a batch system could be unhappy, but terminal users (because they are now working directly with the computer) become more aware of how improvement could be made and make even more change requests than the batch user.

Therefore, requests for a radically different approach to the provision of dp services come not only from users but often from the dp department itself. The impressive cost/performance characteristics of today's small computers (especially minicomputers) can make it very easy for a user department to justify a decentralized system for an isolated application. The dp department might support this; to take the application onto the central site machine might cause an even costlier upgrade. The role of corporate management in this is clear; if the user is talking hard cash and the dp department has no easy answer, then clearance to go ahead would not be unexpected.

Once that breakthrough is made, once a precedent is set, then the trend to more widespread decentralization can be expected. Of course, the first system has to be successful, and the finding of this study is that they almost invariably are (especially if developed by a specialist system house). An interesting feature of these decentralized systems is that they are invariably on-line transaction-processing systems. Nobody wants to go back to batch working. Indeed, it was found in many cases that a desire for an interactive operation (which could not easily be provided by the central mainframe) was a significant criteria in the decision to decentralize.

Situations where there is no interchange of data between remote and central sites are very rare. The very minimum seems to be a weekly or monthly tape of management statistics. Many remote interactive systems rely on the mainframe for bulk batch processing. For lower volumes of data interchange, an off-line medium (magnetic tape or diskettes) is employed. For higher volumes or more frequent transmission dial-up telephone lines might be used. This is a very popular technique now that such transmissions can take place at 2400 bit/s and sometimes 4800 bit/s. Where almost instant connect-time between processors is required the private leased lines are used. More of these technical factors will be dealt with in Chapter 2.

1.4 INFLUENCE OF TECHNOLOGICAL DEVELOPMENTS

We have described above how the process of centralization itself can create an environment which, in turn, creates pressures to decentralize. The trend towards decentralization and the distribution of data processing activities is also stimulated by a number of significant technological developments (Figure 2).

Over the years, terminals have been getting increasingly more "intelligent". There are two primary reasons for this (neither having anything to do with DDP). The first cause relates to the development of plug-compatible terminal devices which would compete directly with those sold by the mainframe suppliers. If you want to emulate the IBM 3270 display system or the ICL 7181 VDU, then it is much easier to do it in software than in hardware. Not only does this keep costs down but it enables the same hardware to be used with a different software emulator to make a product which is plug-compatible with some other suppliers terminal. A similar technique was employed to emulate remote batch terminals such as the ICL 7020, IBM 2780 and Univac 1004.

The second reason for increasing intelligence in terminals is the use of micro-processors (or 'programmable microelectronics') as control mechanisms. The supplier in this case did not necessarily want to emulate anything; the rapidly-decreasing cost of micros just made it the most economical way of building a terminal.

Regardless of the reason for the intelligence, the mere fact that it is there will lead many systems designers to find good use for any spare capacity. Similarly the suppliers of such terminals did not take long to

Figure 2

Influences in the Trend to Decentralization
and
the Distribution of Data Processing

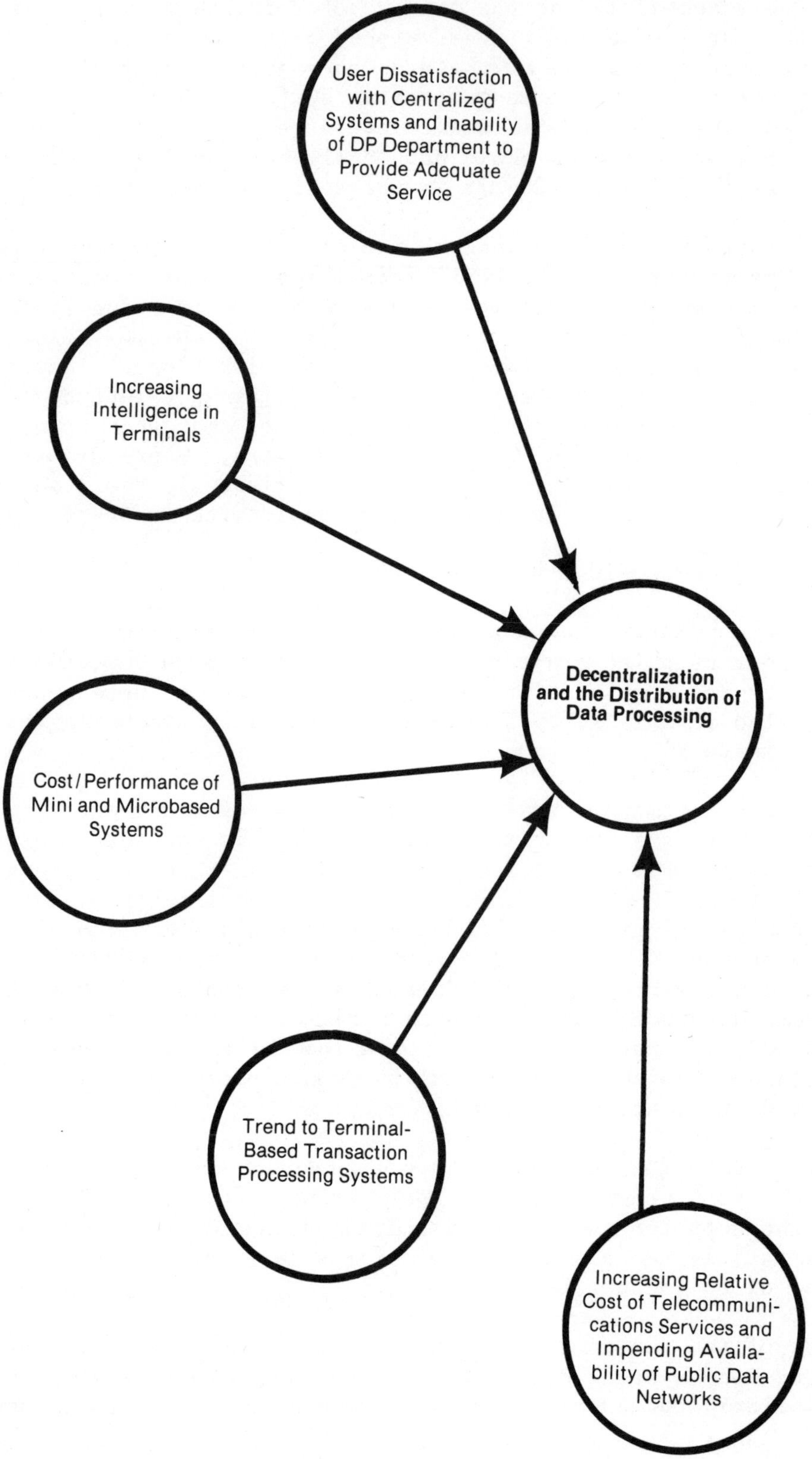

exploit the availability of some, albeit limited, power as a selling point. The processing performed in practice has tended to be limited to simple data checking and screen handling in what was essentially still a centralized teleprocessing network. But it was a start; response-time could be improved, cleaner data sent to the central site and, in the event of line or CPU failure, it might have been possible to do data input off-line for subsequent transmission.

The rapid rate at which the cost of minicomputers has descended over the past few years has astounded all but the most blase dp professional. The power of such machines has increased by similar proportions. In the mid-1960s the maximum main storage on the IBM 360/30 was 64 Kbytes. Today minis are available which can have up to 1 Mbyte of memory. A 64 Kbyte block of storage can be bought for as little as $3,500. A usable mini configuration with 128K of memory and processor power comparable to the IBM 370/138 can be bought for less than $35,000. Even IBM themselves can provide such a minicomputer at such a price. The cost of interfacing communications facilities is also lower; the cost of attaching the first telephone line to a mainframe system is often as much as $44,000, but as little as $700 on a mini. But are minis really cheaper than mainframes on a cost/performance basis when one takes account of software differences? The answer seems to be "yes" and is substantiated further in Chapter 2.

The micro-processor is also having an impact on the trend to decentralization. When used as components, micros are making it easier to produce low-cost and highly flexible communications interfaces and peripheral controllers. We have already described how they can be used for communications control, device control and limited application functions in intelligent terminals. Costs are variable; a typical micro might sell in small quantities for $35 but the larger manufacturers make them for as little as $3.50 - the rest of the price being made up of distribution costs, marketing cost and proft. As an indication of the way in which micro memory prices are going, a US supplier recently claimed that they would be able to supply 1 Mbyte of read-only memory on a single board for less than $1,000 by the end of 1978! Much more of these cost improvements tend to be passed on to the end user than is the case with mainframe-related technology. Small processor developments are significant to the discussion because mini-based systems are more suitable for interactive use than mainframes. A negative factor influencing the trend to decentralization is the cost of tele-communications services. With rare exception, the cost of telephone and telegraph facilities has increased steadily over the past ten years. Where Post Telephone & Telegraph (PTT) charges have remained static, this in itself represents an increase relative to total system costs because of sharp falls in in other areas. For European organizations the problem of international circuits is particularly acute. The annual rental for these is now so high that in many cases they are impossible to cost/justify against equivalent dial-up charges. Such leased lines are now often justified purely on procedural grounds; faster speeds and connect-time, better quality.

In return for these higher charges the PTT have, so far, offered little or nothing in return. The fact that we can now transmit at higher speeds with fewer re-transmissions is entirely attributable to advances in modem technology. (Modems are the devices required to interface digital computer equipment to telephone circuits.) Progress is now evident in some countries in the implementation of public data networks and this issue will be discussed in Chapters 2 and 4. Centralized teleprocessing systems depend heavily on the availablity of communications facilities and, as we have said, these are tending to get more rather than less expensive. Decentralization of dp activities tends to minimize this commitment.

1.5 THE PROs AND CONs OF DECENTRALIZATION

Perhaps one of the most important factors in decentralization is that executive management can see benefits in the decentralization of responsibility and control over all line department activities to the managements of those departments. This might be done as a general corporate strategy within which data processing is only a part. Many companies we spoke to emphasized the need to retain centralized control. But, when pressed, the opinion needed significant qualification. Clearly, there is no way in which the dp department could (or would wish to) control the day-to-day activities of a user department. What was generally meant was that control needed to be exercised over the design, acquisition and use of computer systems to avoid a chaos of ill-conceived and poorly-managed projects. That is quite a different thing. Figure 3 puts into perspective the various advantages and disadvantages of decentralization. Obviously, it is not the right philosophy for all organizations and Chapter 6 of the report goes into this further. Adding up the plus and minus points of each side does not help because the importance to be attributed to each will vary from organization to organization. These will be considered again in Chapter 7 which contains some planning guidelines for management. The concept of distributed processing has very much developed in this environment of increased pressure to decentralize. DDP is about meeting user demands for more effective and responsive systems while avoiding many of the apparent dangers of uncontrolled decentralization.

Further reading, if required, is provided in Supplementary Papers SP1, SP2 and SP3.

Figure 3

Advantages and Disadvantages of Decentralization

	Centralized	Decentralized / Distributed
Advantages	• Economies of Scale • Easier Control of Data Processing Resource • No Compatability Problems (?) • Easier DBMS Control • Eliminate Duplication of Effort • Bigger Pool of Skills • Easier Growth Path • High Power Available if Needed for 'Number Crunching' • Well Understood Approach to Data Processing	• More Adaptable to User Needs • Better Response-Times • Improved Failsafety • Lower Communications Costs • Smaller Increments and Expansion Costs • Less Dependance of Data Processing Department • Better File and DBMS Performance • Low Costs (?) • More Modularity and Flexibility • Better Software for Transaction Processing
Disadvantages	• Lower Failsafety (Unsafe Commitment to Single CPU) • High Cost of Back-Up • Susceptible to Congestion • High Communications Costs • Communications Expensive on Mainframes • Mainframes not as Good as Mini at Communications (?) • Larger Increments for Expansion • Less Adaptable to User Needs • Contention and Performance Problems with Files and DBMS • May Restrict Choice of Terminals	• Duplication of Hardware and Software Leads to Greater Costs • Incompatibility Problems • Field Servicing Problems • Corporate Standards and Control • Problem of Equipment Variety if Data Processing Department is to Maintain Application Software • Problem of Inter-Processor Communications • Quality Control on Distributed Files • Relatively New Philosophy

CHAPTER II

DISTRIBUTED PROCESSING IN PRACTICE

2.1 THE DEFINITION GAME

> *"There are three burning issues of our time:*
> 1. *How many angels can you get on the point of a*
>   *needle?*
> 2. *Who invented peanut butter?*
> 3. *What is distributed processing?"*
>
>   John Kirkley
>   Editor, Datamation

It is somewhat inevitable that the data processing profession should have a predilection for categorizing, classifying and compartmentalizing things-especially things about them in their own line of business. Before starting to write this report, we seriously considered the possibilities of avoiding a definition of "distributed processing" altogether. After all, was it Abraham Lincoln who said:

"If you call a tail a leg, how many legs has a dog?"
"Five?"
"No, four. Calling a tail a leg doesn't make it a leg."

Since distributed systems became a fashionable topic it has only required the incorporation of the most limited microprocessor in a display terminal for a supplier to claim that he has a "distributed processing" product. Certainly, he might have a device which could usefully be employed as a component of a distributed system, but how "programmable" should a remote processor be before we have a proper DDP system? In their NCC book "Why Distributed Computing?" Down and Taylor offer the following definition:

"a distributed system is one in which there are several
autonomous but interacting processors and/or data stores at
different geographical locations".

This is a good starting-point. "Autonomous" seems to be a key word to which we might return. The interaction is probably the characteristic which makes a series of decentralized systems into one distributed system. We would take issue with the qualification about different geographical locations; many of the benefits for decentralization list in Figure 3 could apply to a system distributed among departments within a single building.

Some people approach the problem by listing some of the more important common elements, as in this definition by International Data Corporation:

- a network of processing nodes that are functionally or geographically distributed and that are connected via a communications
  link (or recorded on cassettes or diskettes, then shipped)

- data stored and manipulated at each node so that the database is
  spread through the network but accessible

10

- systems development, hardware and software acquisition under central control so that all pieces function as a network rather than simply as a series of nodes that are interconnected.

That is quite good, but certain care is needed with the term "network". It is important not to confuse distributed systems with communications networks which use processors for switching functions. Indeed a packet network may be described as a "distributed switching network" and might be used within a distributed processing network as a data transport mechanism.

As far as terminology is concerned, we tend to use the expressions:

- distributed systems
- distributed processing
- distributed data processing

interchangeably to mean the same thing. "DDP" is a useful abbreviation. Two further expressions:

- distributed file processing
- distributed database systems

describe particular types of distributed systems and, as we shall discover, most DDP systems do have at least some form of distributed files.

To avoid further confusion, we do not propose to offer our own definition of DDP. We might not, in fact, be able to define a distributed system, but we know one when we see one.

2.2 EXAMPLES OF DISTRIBUTED SYSTEMS

As we have seen from the definitions, some degree of autonomy in remote processor operations seems to be the key to DDP. The archetypal systems we shall now examine all have that characteristic.

2.2.1 PROGRAMMABLE TERMINALS

Programmable terminals have now been around for a long time. Much credit must go to the Burroughs Corporation for their pioneering work in this field. It is arguable that the early UK banking systems (based upon the Burroughs TC500 intelligent terminal) fall short of the right level of autonomy to be properly described as "distributed". However, elements of the technique were well established by such systems. The deciding criteria was probably the absence of any local files (other than data collection).

Today, however, it is possible to obtain programmable terminals which are as powerful as the hosts of 15 years ago. Even more important than processing power is the availability of low cost direct access storage devices such as diskettes and small cartridge disk. A large US corporation has a typical distributed system employing such intelligent terminals. Each area sales office has an IBM 3735 intelligent terminal. The fixed disk in this device contains a simple customer file:

- name and address
- delivery details
- price information

Because of the nature of the company's business no stock file is needed; they have a small product line and are never out of stock. Customers telephone the orders into the sales office. Order details are entered into the terminal which produces complete invoices and delivery notes. At the end of each day, the terminal operator calls the computer centre on the public telephone network and sends details of the days invoices. These are used for overnight updating of the corporate sales ledger. All sales accounting functions are performed on the central batch machine. The benefits of the system are:

- rapid production of delivery notes and invoices
- no centralized data preparation function required
- customer file maintained locally
- low communications cost

This system works well because the amount of information to be transferred between the sales office system and the central system is minimized by the nature of the application. Companies supplying programmable terminals include:

- Harris Corporation
- Datapoint
- Wang
- Incoterm
- IBM
- Burroughs
- Univac

and others. A schematic of DDP system employing programmable terminals is shown in Figure 4. Micro-processors will be used increasingly in this area.

2.2.2 REMOTE PROCESSORS

Figure 5 shows a typical DDP configuration employing remote processors. Unlike the previous example of the use of programmable terminals, these processors are usually able to support a number of interactive devices (usually video terminals) and a greater variety of peripherals. Fixed or exchangeable disk is usually employed in preference to diskette drives. In addition to handling local transaction processing, the processor may also be capable of some limited batch work (especially SPOOLING jobs such as disk-to-print operations). Local reference files (and perhaps even update files) will be held. If these are replicated in the host system then techniques will need to be employed to keep them in step. Input transactions destined for the host will probably be held on data collection files for subsequent batch transmission. Communication to the central site may be over dialed or leased lines. A decision to use leased circuits will depend upon:

Figure 4

Programmable Terminals

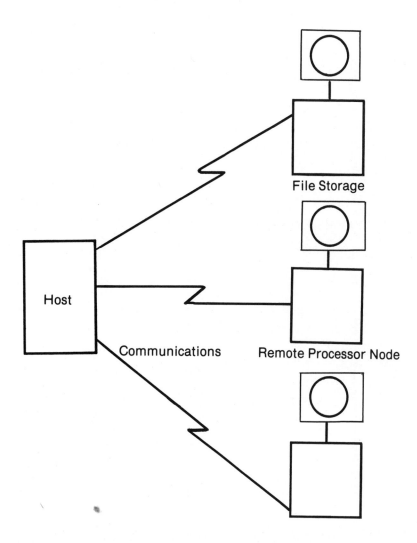

Figure 5

Remote Processors

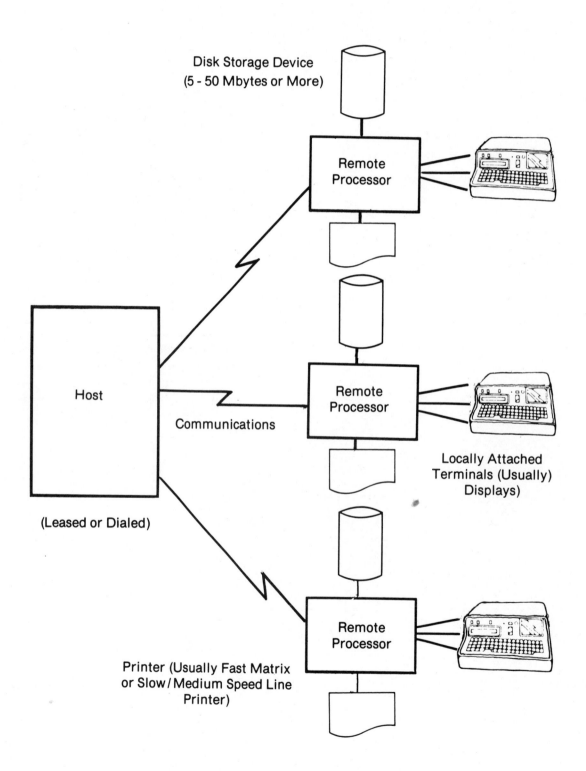

Disk Storage Device
(5 - 50 Mbytes or More)

Remote Processor

Host

(Leased or Dialed)

Communications

Remote Processor

Locally Attached
Terminals (Usually)
Displays)

Remote Processor

Printer (Usually Fast Matrix
or Slow / Medium Speed Line
Printer)

- the volume of transmission between processors
- the need for rapid access (e.g. an enquiry) to a file or database on the host machine.

It is surprising how, in practice, so many distributed systems of this type manage with dial-up very easily.

The remote processors themselves are usually one of three types:

- a small business computer (e.g. IBM System/34, ICL 2903)
- a minicomputer (e.g. DEC PDP-11/34, DG Nova, Prime 300)
- a "packaged" DDP machine (e.g. Datapoint 5500, Harris 1600)

For excellent operational examples of this class of system see Installation Reports IR8, IR9 and IR13 in Volume 2.

2.2.3 PROGRAMMABLE CONCENTRATORS

In the previous example, we considered the type of system where each location had its own processor. For many organizations, however, the work load at each site might not justify the exclusive use of a single computer. This problem can be solved by the sharing of a regional machine as shown in Figure 6.

This technique has many of the advantages of DDP but there are a number of problems.

- The user sites are not able to share printer facilities and, therefore, if VDUs are being used at the distant locations, then a character printer may also be required.

- In some countries, the cost of communications between the user sites and the concentrator may be so high that, as the cost of small computers falls, the organization may find that it has an unfeasible system installed.

- The use of communications facilities may also cause problems relating to contention (if the lines are shared), speed (to go over 1200 bit/s will entail the use of expensive synchronous modems) and availability; in any case, small computers are usually not very good at supporting shared polled lines in this manner.

These alone are good reasons why the technique is not too popular. However, for companies with multinational networks it may be the only solution. At present, international and intercontinental lines are very expensive and to provide links directly from each user site in each country directly to the host could be prohibitive. Small processors can be used, perhaps one per country, as a means of reducing the commitment to high-cost international circuits and, at the same time, to make use of the most economical and reliable communications facilities in each country. If transmission between the national nodes and the host is periodic, then the leased lines can be used for speech or facsimile transmission on a shared basis.

Figure 6

Programmable Concentrators

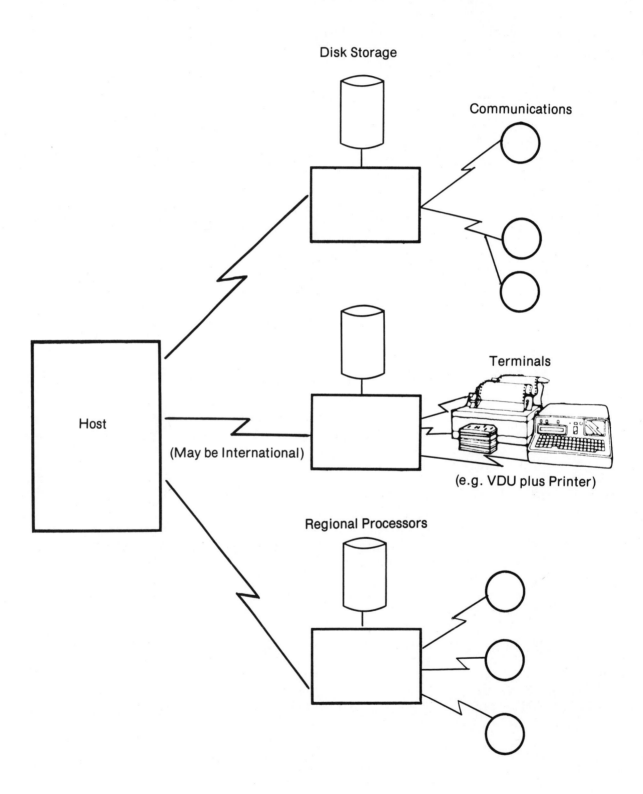

2.2.4 MULTI-LEVEL SYSTEMS

Multi-level DDP systems which involve the use of programmable components at a number of levels could become more common than the technique would appear to justify at first glance. The benefits of DDP would seem to diminish the number of processing levels. However, for some corporate structures (e.g. horizontally integrated corporations such as the Vickers Group - described in IR3) which require the use of quite powerful processors in each division, it may be that each of those divisions has its own communications problem with its remote sites. In some cases, the use of programmable terminals may be the answer (if only for off-line data input and checking). If the divisional computers are linked to the group centre (for loading sharing, corporate database access, etc.), then we have three layers of processing. So what appears to be unduly complex superficially can be well justified in practice. (See Figure 7.)

2.2.5 MULTI-MINI NETWORKS

For the reader not familiar with the basic concepts of minicomputers, we have included an introductory paper on these small, powerful processors, SP7 in Volume 2. The historical development and use of minis in the control system environment means that they are eminently suited to interactive business applications. Their demand-driven architecture contrast sharply with that of mainframe systems which are designed (hardware and software) to provide optimum processing of multiple streams of basic jobs. The relatively high cost of interfacing communications circuits and the need for complex extension to the operating systems (e.g. CICS) are indicative of this weakness.

In an on-line environment, minis are:

- modular
- powerful
- flexible
- adaptable
- reliable

For these reasons, many companies who have used only mainframe computers in the past are developing distributed systems based upon mini processors. In most cases, interfacing to the central site over the communication links will be achieved by having the mini emulate some terminal which is supported as standard by the host. This is by far the most popular technique employed at the present time.

The disadvantage of this is that the CPU still needs to have a communications capability. An alternative approach is illustrated in Figure 8. In this case the mini is connected directly to the host machine's I/O channel and replaces the transmission control unit. Once this is done, teleprocessing software is no longer needed in the mainframe. Usually, special "channel programs" will need to be written in both processors so that data can be passed between them. On some minicomputers, software is now available to emulate suitable batch devices, e.g. magnetic tape drives. This enables the host to treat the whole network as a pair of tape drives

Figure 7

Multi-Level Distributed System

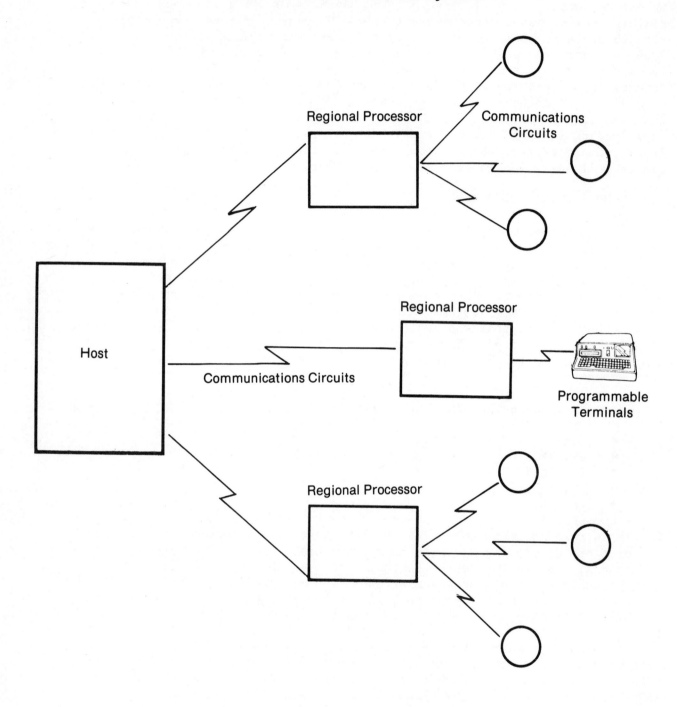

Figure 8

Multiple-Minicomputer Network
(One or More Mainframe Hosts)

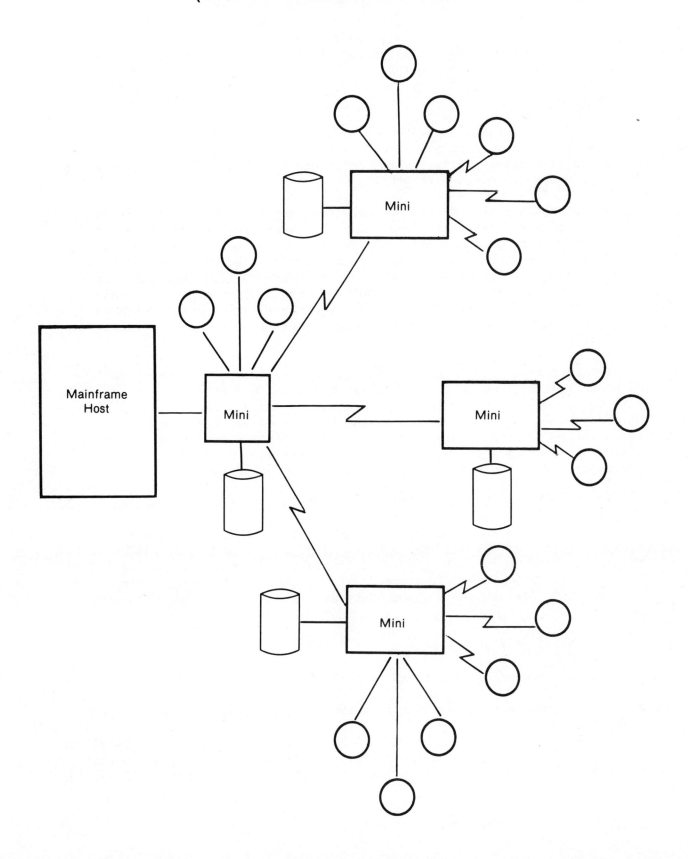

(or whatever). The technique is not quite as simple as that but it is extremely powerful when implemented properly.

Most distributed systems will use mainframe CPUs as hosts. However, the reader might ask whether the mainframe itself could be replaced by minis (if they are all that good!). Such a system is shown in Figure 9.

The viability of this approach is dependent upon the ratio of inter-active processing to batch processing in a given company. The more batch processing done, the more likely you are to have one or more mainframes. However, the general trend to interactive working will make more and more companies consider a mini-only approach; bureau services providing the number crunching.

One of the most well known examples of an organization making a major commitment to minis in this way is Citibank (IR1). (Note: the radical change in corporate structure which proceeded this move will be referred to again in Chapter 6 of this report).

An interesting illustration of the comparative economics of mainframes versus multi-mini systems is provided by the work done by the DP department of the City of Malmo in Sweden. Up until 1972 Malmo had two large Datasaab miniframes, a centralized database and all processing was carried out in batch mode. At that time, the city decided to use on-line terminals for a new application; social welfare payments. This system worked well and gained extensive user acceptance. However, the classic problem with good teleprocessing systems-unexpected growth-caused the Datasaabs to reach capacity by 1974. Malmo was at a crossroad.

The success of the on-line social welfare system was so great that the dp department decided that it was wise to assume that all applications would have to become interactive sooner or later. A design team estimated that the City would eventually need a system capable of handling some 130 transactions/sec. An evaluation of the marketplace showed that no single system was readily available which could handle such a load. A multi-processor system would be needed; but what type of processor?

In the early 1970s there would have been no question that the CPUs would have to be relatively large mainframes. However, over the period of the study, the department became increasingly interested in the potential of minicomputers. It was discovered, for example, that an IBM 370/148 with 2 Mbytes of main memory could handle 10 transactions/sec for a cost of $1.15M. By comparison a typical minicomputer able to handle 4 transactions/sec might cost $46,000. To achieve a throughput rate of 130 transactions/sec would require:

    13 mainframes at a total cost of $1.5M
    or
    32 minicomputers at a total cost of $1.5M

a cost/performance ratio of 10:1 in favor of the mini-based solution.

However, if the balance was that much in favor of minis, nobody would be buying mainframe CPUs any more? Nothing in life is that free... So what are the problems with using minis in this way? As we have discussed earlier

Figure 9

Multi-Mini System (Closely-Coupled and Losely-Coupled)

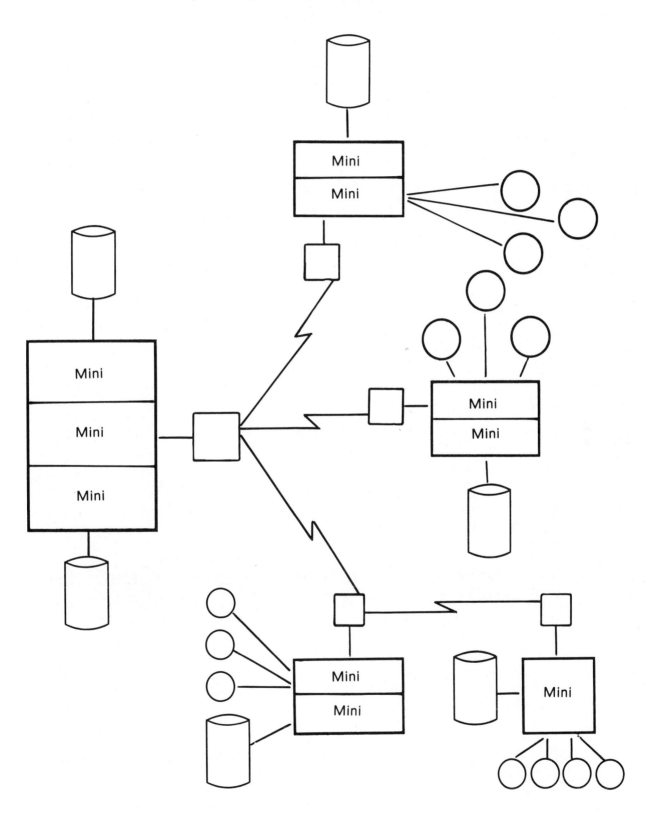

in this report, there are usually two main problem areas for potential commercial users of multi-mini systems:

- effective hardware and software for interconnecting the processors

- suitable software for commercial data processing

The first of these problems was solved for the City of Malmo by their supplier, Data General DG were able to provide a Multiprocessor Communications Adapter to link the computers. (As an illustration of how acute this problem can be, see Installation Report No. 10 on Bank of America.)

The second problem of suitable software was solved by the City of Malmo themselves. Having selected Data General as their supplier, the dp department set up a two-year project to develop their own software. This included:

- a programming language incorporating a display-terminal handler

- extended multiprogramming support

- special communications handlers

- file handling software

- extended multi-terminal handling

It is arguable that if Malmo were starting the same project today then it would be unnecessary to develop much of this software. However, it was necessary at the time and this inevitably reduced the head start the mini-hardware had over the mainframe hardware. But do not forget, on the basis of the cost comparision made above they had over $13M to play with! In September 1977 the City of Malmo had 14 minis and 80 terminals installed. The level of user satisfaction is very high, as is that of the dp department whose far-seeing decision as long ago as 1974 would seem to have been vindicated.

2.3 THE ELEMENTS OF DISTRIBUTED SYSTEMS

Having reviewed the main types of distributed system currently found in practice, it may now be appropriate to specify in a little more detail the main components used to build such networks.

2.3.1 TERMINALS

Terminals can play one of two roles in a distributed system; they can be the remote programmable units or they can provide the means by which users interact with the distributed resource. We have already discussed the use of intelligent terminals in Section 2.2.

By far the most popular terminal for use with remote processors is the visual display. Although some products make use of small-screen special-purpose data-entry stations, the most common approach now being employed uses microprocessor based "teletype-compatible" displays wihich can be made to perform a variety of relatively sophisticated, almost "intelligent", functions under the close control of the shared processor.

Where terminals are remotely sited from the processor these will need to be the orthodox, buffered (and perhaps pollable) devices used in centralized teleprocessing networks. As mentioned in Section 2.2 these may also be programmable if only because it is cheaper to make them with microprocessors than any other way.

It is unusual to find keyboard printers in a distributed system. Users prefer to work with VDUs and, if anything needs printing, a fast printer attached to the processor could be shared. This might not work if users are remotely sited from the processor and, therefore, printers may have to be slaved off the terminals. Clearly this is a more expensive approach.

The low-cost display will continue for some considerable time to be the main device for user interaction with his processor.

2.3.2 REMOTE PROCESSORS

Discounting the use of mainframes, there are three main types of processor available for use in user sites. These are:

- small business computers (SBCs) such as the IBM System/34, ICL 2903 and so on.

- minicomputers such as the DEC PDP-11, Prime 300, Modcomp II and DG Nova.

- Special-purpose distributed processing products like the Datapoint 5500, Harris 1600, IBM 3790 and Univac IT.7.

What are the relative merits of each of these approaches? SBCs are probably one of the easiest ways of implementing a distributed system. The major benefits have been identified as:

- a single-supplier system if SBCs is made by mainframe supplier

- quite good high-level programming languages available (but be wary of RPGII for interactive working!)

- well-defined and supported procedures for data transmission between the SBC mode and the host

- may have packaged software for key-to-disk data input

- good software for local batch processing activities

In contrast with this, there may be a number of fairly major disadvantages:

- limited expansion capability

- inability to support 'foreign' terminals

- inter-processor data transmission limited to batch (no good for enquiries to the host)

- limited support for terminals connected from remote sites over telephone lines

- hardware and software architecture may not be ideal transaction processing

- may only be possible to communicate with the host mainframe and not other processor modes

- lack of ability to share peripherals between two processors may limit failsafety

For many organizations, the SBC may well provide an ideal solution to remote processor requirements. However, few of the installed DDP systems use SBCs, the majority favoring a mini-based solution on a special-purpose product.

The advantages of using minis may be summarized as follows:

- modular, flexible and adaptable configurations (both hardware and software)

- expandable in relatively small increments

- high reliability and capable of being configured for failsafety with shared peripherals and interprocessor links

- 'networking' software (such as DECNET and MAXNET) may provide an efficient means of interconnecting remote nodes

- ability to support a wide variety of terminal types and peripherals

- good communications capability; many lines at a wide range of speeds may be attached (restricted usually by throughput of processor)

- good control programs and software for transaction processing; many minis now have packages (e.g. CA SyFa, Prime's FIRST)

- Use of minis enables orgnizations to benefit quickly from improvements in technology; cheaper memory, faster processors, etc.

Like SBCs, minis have their disadvantages but they are different ones:

- There is a good chance that buying minis will put you in a mixed-supplier situation but this is no longer inevitable now that IBM has the Series/1 and Univac has bought Varian. All mainframe suppliers except CDC, Itel, Amdahl and ICL now offer minicomputers.

24

- Procedures for communicating with the host mainframe may need to be specially developed; alternatively, a software package may be obtained to emulate a host-supported device such as a remote batch terminal.

- If emulation techniques are used for communication between the host and the remote processor this may restrict the type of interaction possible; also many of the remote batch emulators currently available are very inefficient and take up much processor capacity.

- Although it is easy to interface any type of communications faclity to a mini, software support for such functions as polling is relatively rare and may have to be specially commissioned to suit the remote terminals being used.

- Minis do not automatically incorporate all the distributed functions which you may require, and additional effort in this area may need to be budgeted.

It is in this last area that special-purpose DDP products provide a significant advantage. Most such processors (e.g. Harris, Datapoint, Four-Phase, Basic-Four) are in fact minicomputer-based but are packaged by the supplier so that the most commonly used functions are already programmed in. Other benefits include:

- good high-level languages for transaction processing (e.g. Datapoint's Datashare)

- relatively efficient emulators for remote-batch working

- ability to emulate interactive display systems such as the IBM 3270

- support for interleaved batch/interactive transmissions the remote node and the host

- usually single-supplier provision of processor and terminals

This 'packaged' approach certainly seems to work; it is the technique used by the most successful DDP systems visited during this study. Any criticisms tend to be directed at specific products rather than the whole concept and usually relate to restrictions imposed by the packaging.

2.3.3 COMMUNICATIONS

In Chapter 1 of this report it was asserted that the cost of tele-communications services is likely to represent an increasingly large proportion of total system costs. At the moment the problem is not too acute; some work carried out by the author for the UK Post Office between 1973 and 1975 discovered that for small and medium sized teleprocessing systems, the proportion was in the range of 10-20%. However, as the number of remote sites in the system increases, the proportion can rise to as much as 50% depending upon the project write-off period.

The situation over the next ten years is likely to get worse rather than better; even if line charges remain the same, the rapid fall in processor costs alone will cause the communications portion to increase. The increasing number of organizations using international circuits are particularly penalized by the artificially high charges for such lines. Proposals such as those made by the Italian PTT for a volume-based tariff are unlikely to help. We do not believe any of the European PTTs will be prepared to accept lower revenues from this quarter. The US has already seen the introduction of its first public packet-switched service-Telenet. Datapac in Canada and Transpac in France should be operational soon. Spain already has a limited packet service in use and the Dutch, Belgian and Italian PTTs have all announced plans for packet networks. In the United Kingdom the Experimental Packet Switched Service (EPSS) has, in the opinion of author, been an abject failure; it has no commercial users at all. It is anticipated, however, that the UK Post Office will announce the development of a new public data network based upon the CCITT X.25 standard (see SP.6) before the end of 1977.

In Scandinavia, plans are well in hand for a fast digital circuit-switched service, the only one of its kind currently being considered. It would seem though that the Nordic PTTs are getting cold feet over this and are now planning to introduce packet-switching as well.

In the view of the author, it is unlikely that the tariffs for public data networks will be any lower than existing equivalent charges. The services will be sold more on improved speeds, quality of service and new facilities than on cost. In any case, it is likely that some PTTs will introduce regulatory pressures and perhaps punative tariffs on leased lines in order to 'encourage' migration to packet services.

Let us return for a moment to consider existing services and the way in which they are used. Centralized teleprocessing systems almost invariably require the use of dedicated private circuits. DDP seems to have been remarkably successful in avoiding the need for leased lines and making the best use of the public telephone network. A typical node transmits data to and from the host for between 30 and 120 minutes per day at 2400 bit/s. The major limitation of this is that the system has to be designed to avoid the need to make frequent enquires on a host database. Now that transmission on dial-up lines at 2400 and 4800 bit/s is relatively easy to do (subject to the quality of the lines), this technique will be a popular approach in distributed systems.

On the other hand, the use of packet networks would seem to be ideally suited to DDP for the following reasons:

1. access is always available for interactive working to the host (e.g. for database enquiries)

2. speed is available for bulk transmission

3. any node connected to the network can talk to any other node without going through the host

4. the non-transparent nature of packed nets makes it easier to have networks of mixed suppliers

5. network expansion is eased; the addition of a new node might be handled by an existing high-speed packet interleaved port at the host

6. a volume-sensitive tariff should, hypothetically, help to reduce costs and control budgets

As the reader will have gathered, we are enthusiastic about the potential for DDP users of packet networks. However, we are very unhappy about the X.25 Standard for interfacing to packet networks which has been agreed at CCITT. Our feeling is that it is unnecessarily expensive and cumbersome. This view is elaborated further in the Technical Report (Volume 2).

2.3.4 THE HOST SYSTEM

Although clear patterns are emerging in the use of distributed processors, the role of the host and its future is less clear. The problem is illustrated by the wide disparity of 'hosts' in the systems surveyed by this project. In some cases (e.g., The City of Malmo) it is unclear whether there is a host as such. Many multi-mini systems could be 'acentral' in structure. The Citibank Fund Transfer System (IR1) does have a central machine but is not a host (in the sense of acting as the central controlling device in the network); it merely acts as a message-switch between the nodes. In contrast with this, the IBM approach to DDP (embodied in SNA-see Section 3) is heavily dependent on the host computer.

The need for a host and its resultant size will be dependent upon such factors as:

- the amount of batch processing required
- the need for a number-cruncher
- the requirement for a centralized corporate database
- the requirements of any 'network architecture' being used
- the politics of the organization concerned

Beyond this, it is difficult to generalize. It does seem however that the majority of DDP systems:

- will retain a host
- will use a mainframe processor for this
- will be less susceptible to 'uncontrolled' growth in mainframe size

If management desires to minimize host requirements this could color attitudes to network architectures such as SNA. This matter will be discussed further below and in Chapter 3.

2.3.5 NETWORK ARCHITECTURES

In the simplest of terms, 'network architectures' are a set of rules which, when implemented in a DDP environment, can act as the 'glue' which holds the system together. These architectures usually comprise:

1. a data link control which can be used to pass data from one processor to another

2. a 'high level protocol' which is an interprocessor command language

3. the hardware and software products needed to implement the above

The high-level protocol can enable a program in one processor to:

- send data to a program in another processor
- access a file in another processor
- cause a program to be executed in another processor
- initiate the bulk transfer of data between processors
- and so on

The detailed network configuration will be transparent to the program.

Network architectures are a good thing. They ease the development of distributed systems and provide a range of useful facilities. Unfortunately, at the present time these architectures are developed by manufacturers for use on their own systems. This makes life difficult for the user of mixed systems. However, the British Standards Institute and the International Standards Organization have started work on the development of a standard High Level Protocol which could be used between a variety of computers. This is probably one of the most important developments in the field of standardization today. Volume 2 of this report contains descriptions of two network architectures: SNA and Digital Equipment's DECNET.

2.4 ECONOMIC CONSIDERATIONS

Some of the most useful work done to date on the cost aspects of distributed systems was carried out by Peter Down and Frank Taylor of the UK National Computer Centre (NCC). This work is reported in their books "Why Distributed Computing" (NCC Publications 1976). The work done in this project has tended to confirm their original assumptions and, therefore I shall borrow heavily from their publications.

A word of warning, however. The purpose of this exercise is to illustrate the relative cost structures of comparable system solutions employing varying degrees of distribution. It does not provide a means of costing individual systems; this can only be done in the context of a particular organization's development and operational environment. For example, programming costs in Scandinavia are twice as high as in the UK. Leased line charges in France are about twice the cost for the same distance as in the USA. The need for international circuits will also distort the picture.

The only answer is for the organization to design for itself a variety of solutions, perhaps ranging from a centralized teleprocessing system to a completely decentralized configuration. An example of this approach is documented in IR15 (Volume 2). An indication of the scale of costs encountered in practice can be obtained from the Installation Reports.

The best way of approaching the analysis of cost structures is to start categorizing system costs into three main areas:

1. Remote Site
   This includes terminals, remote processors, associated peripherals and development costs (including programming).

2. Communications
   This is a combination of circuit rental or usage charges along with lease or purchase costs for other components such as modems and multiplexors.

3. Central Site
   This covers the purchase or lease costs of central site components such as processors, peripherals, design and software development, network control centres and so on. There are many other items which are difficult to allow for. Take, for example, the question of the cost of office space. A typical view expressed by many designers was that DDP can ease space requirement at the computer centre which tends to be expensive because of the need for special flooring, air conditioning, power supply backup, security and so on. But if this space exists already it is unlikely to disappear. Quite often the costs of space for the remote processors is not allowed for in feasibility studies because of the ability of the locations concerned to 'find space'. That is acceptable in most cases but could be an unsafe assumption where processors are, for example, being installed in retail stores at high-rental city-centre locations.

Generalizing as far as we can, then, Figure 10 illustrates the effect on costs in the three areas identified above for degrees of distribution ranging from the totally centralized (0) to a fully decentralized (1).

As one might expect, the cost of remote site processors and terminals increases steadily as the system becomes more distributed. On the other hand, both communications costs and central site costs both decrease steadily until they reach zero for a totally distributed system. Combining this notional curves together (as in Figure 11) enables one to get a picture of how total costs change with the degree of distribution. This shows how the minimum cost solution often involves some degree of distribution; maximizing the decentralizations does not serve to minimize costs. Of course the shape of the total cost curve will vary from case to case and some intermediate options might cause it to rise unexpectedly.

The reader should note that a major finding of this study was that the cost of developing software for processors was much less than anticipated; see Installation Reports IR9, IR8 and IR6.

An assessment of the effect of technological developments on this cost structure is dealt with in Chapter 4.

Figure 10

Effect of Distribution on System Costs

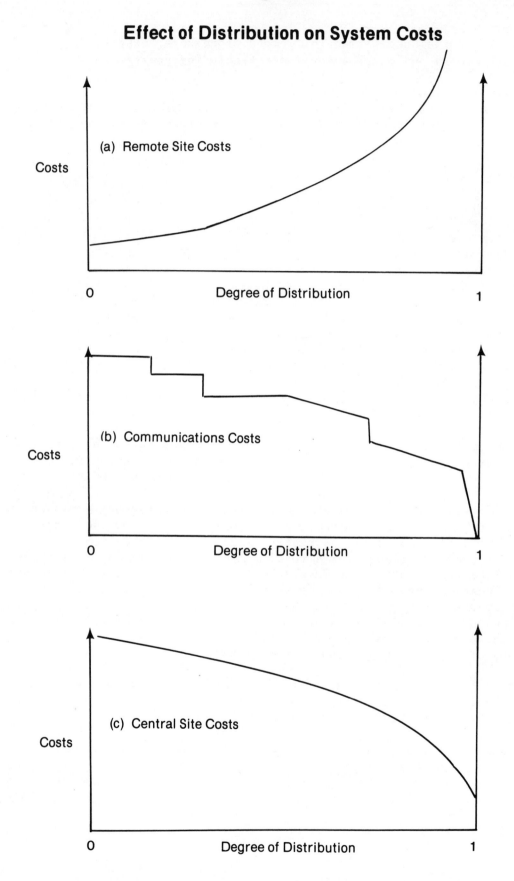

(a) Remote Site Costs

Costs

0   Degree of Distribution   1

(b) Communications Costs

Costs

0   Degree of Distribution   1

(c) Central Site Costs

Costs

0   Degree of Distribution   1

Figure 11

Cost Structure of Distributed Systems

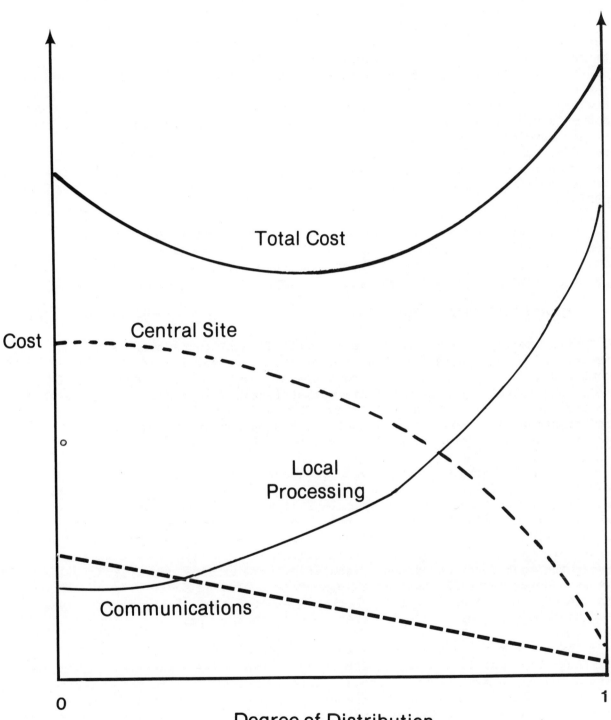

CHAPTER III

THE IBM SCENE

3.1 INTRODUCTION

The purpose of this section of the management report is to assess
current developments and attitudes in IBM with respect to data communications in general and distributed data processing in particular. IBM's
approach to DDP is bound to have some impact on the extent to which users as
a whole accept the distributed approach; if IBM does it well then DDP could
develop rapidly; if, on the other hand, IBM does it badly then... It is the
author's view that IBM's somewhat costly and cumbersome implementations of
teleprocessing in the past have served to slow down the acceptance of
terminal-based systems. This effect has only been encountered in recent
years when minicomputer suppliers have shown how very simple and inexpensive
it can be to attach a terminal to a computer. Will the same thing happen to
DDP?

Distributed processing with IBM is based upon Systems Network
Architecture (SNA). This 'package' of hardware and software products is
described briefly and its likelihood of success from both external and
internal competition is assessed.

3.2 IBM AND DISTRIBUTED PROCESSING

What exactly is IBM's attitude to DDP? I think the answer is best
summarized as a reluctant recognition of the inevitability of the trend
combined with a determination to control the degree of distribution as a
means of protecting their mainframe marketplace. This conclusion is reached
on the basis of discussions with many IBM staff in Europe and top US,
conversations with consultants knowledgeable on IBM issues and an
examination of various internal IBM papers on DDP.

Two particular documents provide the most interesting insight to IBM
thinking. The first is a marketing guide on Distributed Processing which
was first produced by IBM domestic in 1976 as a briefing document for
branch salesmen and SEs. We will refer to this as the 'Marketing Guide'
(IBM's reference is ZZ20-3829 but we do not know whether the Guide is
available outside the US). The second document is a report by a software
marketing task force based upon discussions earlier this year (1977) with
about a dozen major IBM customers in America including Eastman Kodak, Exxon,
Martin Marietta, Equitable Life, Morgan Guaranty Trust, Phillips Petroleum
and McDonnel Douglas. We will refer to this as the 'Task Group Report'.

The third paragraph of the Marketing Guide makes a fairly clear
statement of what IBM considers DDP to be: "Many companies have gone in the
direction of centralized processing, while some have gone in the direction
of decentralized processing. Certainly there are advantages to both, yet
the disadvantages of both are causing many companies to look for a better
solution. Distributed Processing as a concept, is a marriage of the two,
with the objective of capitalizing on the advantages and eliminating many of
the disadvantages of the purely centralized approaches. It is a concept
designed to accelerate application growth with more user flexibility in

systems design and operation, without the loss of adequate corporate controls. It is a concept consistent with IBM's Systems Network Architecture and a concept supported by present hardware and software."

So far so good (Systems Network Architecture-SNA-will be considered later). The Guide then goes on to describe the history of DP developments through decentralization, centralization to centralized teleprocessing (as was done in Chapter 2 of this report).

At this point, the Guide postulates the view that the major influence in the trend towards distributed systems lies with user department pressure for new and improved applications on a dp department which is unable to respond because of existing maintenance and development workloads. As users become more educated in dp and learn about what is possible, it is inevitable that they will demand better quality systems, more usable systems. If the dp department is unable to provide these requirements they will find it difficult to resist user decisions to acquire packaged or semi-packaged solutions from external sources such as systems houses. If such solutions fail then the resultant mess may have to be cleared up by the dp department. If the solution succeeds, then this will be a spur to further 'illicit' developments in both the originating and other departments. This will cause loss of corporate control (the Guide claims) and failure to benefit from sharing development costs. A split will arise between dp and the user departments.

IBM's major concern with this trend (as expressed in the Guide) is that if a split does occur, the user will tend to identify the IBM salesman as being 'on the side of the dp department' thereby leaving the competition to get into the user department directly and make sales. In other words, the Guide sees decentralization as the major threat and distributed processing as a means of meeting user demands and at the same time retaining control of the situation. The arguments made for and against the centralized/ decentralized approach are reasonably sound ones:

Centralized

Advantages. One of the key objectives of installing data processing has always been to reduce costs. The centralized approach helps limit redundant costs in people, hardware, software, data space requirements and other areas. It has the objective of maximizing resource sharing of people, hardware, software, data, as well as experience. It provides a system that may be easier to manage and control a real plus in this rapidly growing environment.

Disadvantages. In many cases, the disadvantages of such a system have come from overuse of the advantages. For example, overcontrol may force rigidity in standards and scheduling on the user. It may have decreased responsiveness and made tailoring more difficult. It may make costing and justification difficult for the user to understand. Systems reliability is readily apparent to all users, who may become less tolerant as their ability to work without the system decreases. Finally, there is an overhead in systems and in personnel that is also readily apparent and does not offset some of the potential savings in the elimination of redundancy mentioned above.

Decentralized

Advantages. The key advantages of this approach normally accrue to the user, and this is why the user generally supports the alternative when the centralized approach fails to meet expectations. This approach can give the user increased control over the operation of the system and can increase the ability to tailor the system to the user's desires. It can provide independence from the DP organization. In addition, it can make it easier for the user to understand the costing and billing of the application. The user may view this approach as more reliable even though it may not be. Additionally, the user may be more motivated to participate in the implementation of new applications.

Disadvantages. Many of the disadvantages do not appear until the system has been installed for some time. They arise not from the initial plan, but from growth either in the installed applications or in the number of applications handled by the systems, there is also the potential problem of redundancy in hardware, software, personnel and experience. In addition, there can be a problem in transferring work, people, skills, data and programs between systems, partly because of system incompatibilities and partly because of lack of standards. Finally, this approach can increase the difficulty of managing standards, backup, duplicate data, programming, communications control, security, privacy, growth and many more items.

Most people would agree that that is a fair assessment of the situation. However, the Guide then makes a quantum jump to the statement that:

> "The objective...of Distributed Processing is to capitalize on today's centralized database systems and provide the functions required by the users to help them better perform their jobs, improve productivity and decrease costs."

Ignoring the obvious point that the majority of users do not have a 'database system' (centralized or otherwise) this statement runs contrary to the view expressed to me by almost all the DDP users surveyed that their objectives were (among others):

- to benefit as much as possible from the attractive cost/benefit ratio of small computers (especially minis)

- to minimize the commitment to the centralized mainframe

To start out, as IBM does, with the assumption that the mainframe will always be fundamental to distributed systems is unsafe. It is certainly the case that the majority of DDP systems will have some form of mainframe in them (e.g. for batch work) but it should not be taken as a foregone conclusion. The Citibank Corporate Fund Transfer System (Installation Report No. 1) does, for instance, have a central computer but its role as a data switch between the divisional processor is so minimal that only a minicomputer is required.

This emphasis on protecting the mainframe is perpetuated throughout the Marketing Guide. The DP salesman is told that:

"A point to be emphasized is that the basic concept of centralized data base (sic) and centralized control is not being changed."

Who says so? For some applications and some organizational structures decentralized control over decentralized data bases might be the ideal solution. The Guide does concede that decentralization might lead to a reduction in mainframe needs but claims that total expenditures will be greater:

"With the potential for CPU cost reduction in Distributed Processing systems, IBM revenue growth is dependent on successfully marketing IBM terminal products to satisfy distributed function requirements."

But the fact that IBM would prefer its revenue to come from the 'safer' CPU area is underlined by design guidelines drawn up by the 'Task Group':

"Choice between central and DDP should be:

- central when local function can be moved to central site

- central when local function data base cannot be localized

- local when local function cannot be centralized and data can be localized also"

This very negative approach is, again, contrary to the consensus view of the many DDP users I have spoken to. This view may be summarized as: "if it makes sense, procedurally and financially, to localize a function, then localize it". In its conclusions, the Guide summarizes IBM's view of DDP thus:

"It is important (for the DP salesman) to stress the 'system solution'. The central DB/DC system approach was the direction in the past and is still the heart of the system. It is the base of a Distributed Processing system solution. DB/DC is still the key. Distributed Processing is not a new radical direction but rather a logical follow-on to DB/DC. The Distributed Processing direction is consistent with the past centralized direction yet recognizes the realities of the user department desires not now being responded to by the centralized approach. SNA provides the architecture to implement this solution, and the 3790, along with the other IBM products, provides the product line to implement this solution."

That is the IBM view, but the reality of DDP today is different. Of course, many installations will introduce an element of programmability into the network of what is essentially a centralized system in order to provide better user services and so on. In other cases, however, the introduction of DDP has represented a radical departure from the traditional approach (e.g. Gulf Atlantic Distributed Services, Pacific Stereo, Citibank, Norwegian State Railways, Elida Gibbs).

As stated in the last quotation (above) from the Guide, IBM's approach to DDP is based upon SNA and this is discussed in the next section.

3.3 SYSTEM NETWORK ARCHITECTURE

The way in which we have implemented teleprocessing systems in the past (and to an extent, still do) has been nothing short of a mess:

- the use of telephone lines is crude and inefficient

- special (and often non-standard) software is needed for some applications or terminals

- many low-level control functions need to be handled in application programs

- application programs are difficult to maintain and largely unportable

- it is difficult to 'grow' the system by adding terminals, files, circuits, etc.

- operating systems are not suited to terminal-based environments and need to be extended by using software such as CICS

It must be said that this problem is by no means unique to IBM.

More than three years ago now, IBM announced Systems Network Architecture (SNA). This, in brief, is:

- a set of design rules for all future communications related products

- a set of hardware and software products

- a 'direction setting concept' to help IBM customers in the long-term planning of their communication systems

(A detailed description and assessment of SNA is included as Supplementary Paper No. 5.)

Although SNA does support distributed processing (as well as centralized teleprocessing) it does not, on its own, support distributed data bases or load sharing amongst CPUs. Another level of software (e.g., IMS) and/or user-written programs need to be added to achieve these functions. When IBM first announced SNA they were quite firm that the new corporate standard would be imposed quite strictly on all new products. Only in this way could users be assured that the direction set would not encounter any crossroads. SNA is based upon the following 'products':

- a single telecommunications access method (TVAM)

- a programmable communications control unit (the 370X) with appropriate software (Network Control Program-NCP)

- a single data link control (SDLC)

- a range of programmable terminal systems (the 3790 general purpose programmable display system, the 3600 Finance Communications Systems, 3650 Retail Store System, etc.)

The benefits claimed for the SNA approach include:

- the off-loading of control and application functions from the CPU to the control units and terminals

- network transparency

- terminal device independence

- reduced communications costs through line-sharing, reduced message traffic and full-duplex (simultaneous both way) transmission

- single shared general-purpose access method

- improved response times and throughput (especially with mixed interactive and batch transmissions)

- multiple-host support

- standard, general-purpose data link control for all terminals

- reduced application program development costs

That, in brief, is the case for SNA. IBM's overt or 'public' motives in wanting to 'tidy up' the teleprocessing scene and to aid customers' medium to long-range planning is nothing less than laudable. However, many people we spoke to during the study believe that IBM has a number of other motivations and these will be considered further in Section 3.5 below.

Ignoring for the time being the problem of motivation, let us now consider the disadvantages of SNA as reported both by users and by companies who have evaluated it and rejected it. These disadvantages may be summarized as follows:

- increased main storage requirement (in most systems?)

- increased CPU overhead (in some systems?)

- increased transmission controller costs

- no support for the Integrated Communications Adapter

- no Advanced Communications Functions support for the 3704

- increased modem costs (must be synchronous)

- no HASP support (must migrate to JES)

- limited programmability in remote processors

- poor low-level programming language in the 3790

- no cluster node-to-cluster node communications (always routing via the host may put an unnecessary load on the CPU)

- increased training costs (up to $2,000 per capita) plus pay increases to retain trainees?

- high cost of 'learning curve' for early users (there is little field experience, even in IBM)

- high cost of interfacing non-IBM terminals

- unsuitability of architecture for use of packet-switching networks

A number of these points are worth amplifying. One large SNA installation visited had 1500 logical units (approximately equivalent to terminal devices) connected via 160 cluster nodes and 20 multipoint lines to a 370/168 at the centre. We expected the main storage requirement of VTAM to be reasonably big, but our conversation with the company's senior technical manager went as follows:

"What is the working-set size for VTAM?"

"Three megabytes."

"No, I don't mean the total CPU size, just VTAM."

"Three megabytes!"

"OK. How big is the machine?"

"Four megabytes."

"But aren't you doing any paging?"

"Not much. The virtual size of VTAM is not much more than three megabytes, but if we increase the paging, then the response-times become unacceptable."

We would be the first to accept that this installation may be an extreme case, but some of the main storage requirements quoted in the Supplementary Paper on SNA, indicate that the storage needed to be allocated in most VTAM systems (regardless of size) is a good deal more than has been allocated in pre-SNA systems. Other SNA products are also more costly than has previously been the case.

The structure of SNA also makes it difficult to interface terminal products supplied by companies other than IBM. Clearly, IBM may not be unduly concerned by this but it is important from the user's point of view. Market requirements are so varied in this area that it is becoming increasingly difficult for any single supplier (including IBM) to support a terminal product range able to meet the needs of all possible users. Independent terminal suppliers have been extremely slow to produce systems

(e.g., 3790 emulators) to run in an SNA environment. A variety of reasons
for this were given to me. For example:

- If the 3790 is not a good product (as the 3270 clearly is) why emulate it?

- If IBM is unable to sell SNA, how are we going to sell 3790s?

- Just too risky for the high costs involved

If the terminals to be attached are not 'architected' then there is
little point in using VTAM. By far the most popular approach to DDP at the
moment involves the use of packaged or semi-packaged mini-based remote
processors which are only connected to the host for short periods at the
beginning and end of the day. Despite the deficiencies of present remote-
batch protocols, these seemed to work well enough in the systems surveyed.

Another major criticism of SNA is that the implementation seems to be
suitable for large users only. The ICA Definition is not supported (even
though a special version of VTAM was written for this at the Hursley Labs in
the UK). The most recent release of VTAM/NCP for Advanced Communication
Function also excludes the smaller communications controller node, the
3704. It is arguable that many small users stand to gain more from DDP than
the larger ones. Upgrades to the central-site might be harder to justify
than the use of programmable terminals at the remote sites. Also, the
question needs to be asked as to whether SNA can ever become the standard
for IBM teleprocessing and DDP if it is so difficult to cost-justify by as
many as 80% of IBM's existing customers? The question to be asked is: "Are
the benefits of SNA worth the cost?" Many potential SNA-users are saying
'no'.

Most commercial data communications systems are very homogeneous in
nature. Often a single terminal-type is used throughout the network and
stays the same for the whole project life. Each terminal tends to be
connected to the same application program for hour after hour. Sometimes
the only variability occurs when a terminal uses a dial-up line because its
leased connection has failed.

If the SNA approach is not found to be cost/effective then other
solutions will be sought and found. One of the most interesting features of
the IBM scene currently is the fact that the corporation's own Series/1
minicomputer has an enormous potential to be competitive with the 'official'
teleprocessing product range.

Yet another area of conflict relates to the very rapid development
throughout the world of Public Data Networks using packet-switching
technology. Packet networks seem to be ideally suited to DDP (see
Section 2). The conflict arises because SNA is designed to be operated with
very simple data transmission facilities which, in essence, provide the
nodes with means of moving single bits from one location to another. The
control of the flow of messages between nodes is performed entirely by the
nodes themselves. On a packet-switched network, however, the message (or
'packet') routing and control functions are performed within the networks.
This causes a number of problems. For example, two lots of routing

.information need to be transmitted (one header for SNA, one for the packet net). SNA transmission procedures are based upon having the host node 'poll' the remote devices to give them clearance to transmit; such polling messages will have to be transmitted as packets and the user will be billed for them. IBM has already announced RPQ products to enable the 3790 to transmit over an X.25 packet network to a 3705 controller node. This solution appears to be cumbersome and expensive. It does not allow users to exploit the full benefits of packet switching.

3.4 THE SERIES/1 MINICOMPUTER

The Series/1 mini is probably the most important computer system IBM has announced since the System/360. The Series takes the corporation into the minicomputer marketplace in a sector which is growing about four times as rapidly as the mainframe area. As we have considered elsewhere in this report, the minicomputer has had a major impact on data communications and, many would claim, has been instrumental in the early successes of DDP.

The Series/1 is described and assessed in detail in Supplementary Paper No. 8. A summary view of the products follows:

- sound architecture with good expansion capability

- limited range of peripherals at present but likely to expand significantly with new products from both IBM and the dp industry

- some interesting software features (including a 'do-it-yourself' operating system) but disturbing variations between versions of the Real-time Programming System (RPS)

- Macro-Assembler, FORTRAN and PL/1 are 'official' programming languages, but COBOL, RPG11 and BASIC already announced by software houses

- communications features generally good but weak on one or two specific points

- prices competitive with the rest of the mini marketplace

In the past, IBM has sold the SNA concept as an alternative to the 'proliferation of minis' within a company. But does this argument apply to the Series/1? The Series/1 is developed and marketed by the General Systems Division (who also produced the System/3, /32, /34, etc.). GSD has already announced software packages which enable the Series/1 to emulate two of the Data Processing Division's terminal products; the 3270 and the 3780. Understandably, many senior managers in DP Division were very angry about this development; they have problems enough with Plug Compatible Machine products from outside the corporation!

But the potential is much greater than this. It is possible, to configure remote processors using the Series/1 for as much as 40% cheaper than 3790 equivalents. In addition, the Series/1 could be an alternative to the 370X communications controller if a 370-Series/1 adapter becomes available. This seems likely; during my visit to the Series/1 development centre at Boca Raton in Florida, we were told that many RPQs had been received for such an adapter. If IBM does not produce this device then the dp service industry is certain to. When this happens it will be possible to develop quite sophisticated DDP networks without using any items from the Data Processing Division's range of products.

3.5 SNA CONSIDERATIONS

The following points should be taken into consideration by any organization planning to go to DDP with IBM.

1. Long-Term Planning

IBM's claim is that SNA is most cost-effective when viewed as a sound base for the medium to long-term development of an organization's data communications needs. This assertion is, to a fair extent, speculative. It presumes that SNA products will always be available (or producible) to meet ongoing needs. This may not always be true; for example, no word-processing system is currently obtainable which will operate on an SNA network.

It is important for management to make every attempt to draft a long-term (twenty years?) strategy of likely terminal, remote processor, communications and application requirements. Only in this way can the significance and possible benefits of SNA features and facilities be assessed.

2. Design Alternatives

The benefits of SNA may be very attractive to you. But do not forget that SNA is not the only way of achieving those objectives. A number of suppliers offer alternative approaches. For example, COMTEN in the USA offers its own network system (hardware and software) which provides most of the benefits without going to VTAM/NCP. At a lower level Computer Dynamics Inc., offers software to support the 3790 which, they claim is more efficient than VTAM. Alternatively you may produce your own general-purpose or special-purpose network using minicomputers (perhaps the Series/1).

Only by designing and costing alternative systems will you have a means of assessing the feasibility of the SNA approach.

3. Technical Advice

In spite of IBM's determination to sell SNA at an executive management level there are many detailed technical issues that must be included in the evaluation. For example, it has already been pointed out that the use of packet-switching networks by SNA-based systems is likely to be cumbersome and expensive. This likely problem needs to be viewed in the context of the widespread implementation of packet nets over the next ten years. Even if you do not consider that this technique is relevant to your needs, the PTTs may well raise leased-line charges to punative levels in order to force users over to the new networks. There are many other such technical issues. The point being made is that management should take technical advice before making a decision to go ahead with SNA. The advice must, of course, be well informed.

4. Variability

Generally speaking, the more static and unchanging your terminal system will be, the less you will benefit from SNA. The converse is also true; the more heterogeneous your network, the greater the variety of terminal types and network arrangements, the more likely you are to benefit from the SNA approach. But take care; the size of VTAM is proportional to the variety of network components.

5. Mixed-Supplier Problems

If you are likely to obtain terminals or remote processors from a source other than IBM then you should anticipate problems with the development and commissioning of the emulator (if they are to work in an SNA environment). This is especially so if you will be the first user. If you already have a lot of communications-related terminals and processors installed and want to link these together, then SNA is unlikely to provide a viable solution. The cost of doing what may be a whole series of one-off solutions could be prohibitive. In short, if you are going SNA, then think twice (or three times) about attaching non-IBM terminals. If you have now (or are likely to have) a mixed-supplier situation, then think twice (or three times) about using SNA.

6. The SNA Path

If you do decide to take the SNA approach a few precautions may be necessary:

- you may well be pioneering; adjust your budgets and time-scales accordingly

- if you can get IBM to make some contractual undertakings about performance (particularly VTAM main storage requirements)

- if possible, try SNA on a limited trial system initially; it may not prove anything, but if it does, it could be easier to back out of than a major commitment

- as mentioned previously, the use of PCM terminals could add to your technical problems out of all proportion to the cost savings; if you have to pioneer on SNA do not pioneer on emulators at the same time

So where does that leave us? Howard Frank, President of Network Analysis Corporation has gone on record as saying that SNA cannot survive 'beyond the next few years'. He describes the architecture as 'inflexible' and 'archaic'. We tend to agree; IBM does not always get things right and this is something they have got wrong. SNA is not as good as it could be (neither concept nor products) and is not flexible and adaptable enough to meet users' communications needs in the 1980's.

We do not, however, believe that SNA will die as rapidly as Howard Frank suggests. IBM has put too much resource into it for that. The question to be asked is, how much more successful will SNA become? By IBM's own standards SNA must already be considered a failure. It is well over three years since the concept was first announced and worldwide installations are estimated at 85, but less than half of these are fully operational (rather than experimental) systems. There are two in the United Kingdom and five in Scandinavia.

We feel that SNA will be as successful as IMS, i.e.:

- there will be relatively few users and these will tend to be larger IBM customers

- it will not become an industry standard nor even an IBM standard in terms of customer acceptance

- in many installations, it will not replace existing techniques (e.g., the use of 3780 emulation to connect remote processors)

If the growth of SNA is not stunted by its own limitations, then the widespread development of public packet-switched networks will limit its usability. We mentioned earlier that many people believe that IBM has ulterior motives for SNA. These include:

- 'locking out' PCM terminal suppliers

- countering the development and acceptance of packet-switched networks

- countering the trend to decentralization (that is substantiated in Section 3.2 above)

In trying to counter such trends in computers and communications rather than responding to them, IBM could be on the losing side. Public Data Networks are developing rapidly and the attractive cost/performance ratio of minicomputers has been recognized by IBM itself.

CHAPTER IV

FUTURE TRENDS

*What are the likely future
trends in technology cost/performance
and how will they affect the attractiveness
or otherwise of DDP?*

4.1 REMOTE SITE

There are three main components of remote site systems which
need to be considered:

- Terminals
- Processors
- Peripherals (especially direct access storage and printers)

It is hard to see how the rapid drop in the cost of terminals can
continue as it has done over the past ten years; but it is likely to do just
that. Over the last five years, the price of a simple display that might be
used as a terminal station on a minicomputer has dropped from $2500 to
$1500. This trend could continue until until such a device costs as little
as $1000 by 1990. Terminals with a larger number of electro-mechanical
components will not drop as quickly as this.

At present, most distributed processors are based upon minicomputers.
However, as microprocessors become more and more powerful, many small
'minis' will be replaced. This is already happening with the introduction
of the DEC LS1-11 and DG Micronova. A typical price for an 8-bit micro is
$40 ($60 for a 16-bit device). This does, of course, require 'packaging'
but one could expect the end user price of small processors (micro-based or
not) to drop by 80% between now and 1990. The use of micros in I/O device
control boards is already an established technique and will further serve to
reduce costs. The cost of processors is dropping so rapidly that cost of
memory is becoming of increasing importance. However, the cost of memory
is, if anything, dropping even more rapidly than processors (Figure 12).
This process has been helped by the replacement of core storage with
solid-state memory (Figure 13). These amazing trends will continue, but it
is not known how far. The cost of interfacing to communications lines has
dropped from over $2000 per line to as little as $400 per line and could
continue on to $200, (especially if digital communications networks enable a
simpler interface to be used).

The decline in cost of peripherals such as disk and printers will be
steady, much less dramatic. Reduction in the region of 50% (in
cost/Megabyte) should be expected. This prediction will, hopefully, be
invalidated by a breakthrough into cheap, mass storage devices. Bubble
memory technology looks promising but opinion seems to be divided about the
viability of producing 10 Mbytes exchangeable 'blocks' for about $3500 each.

Figure 12

Semiconductor Random Access Memory Trends

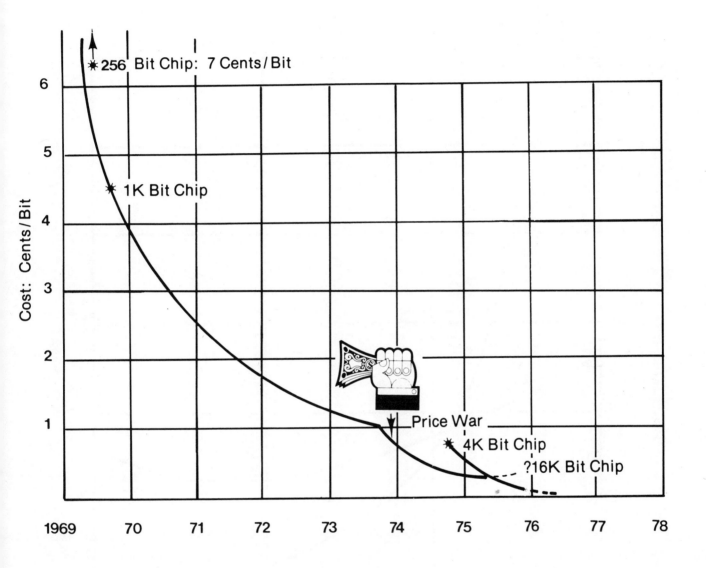

Figure 13

Memory Costs: Core vs. Semiconductor

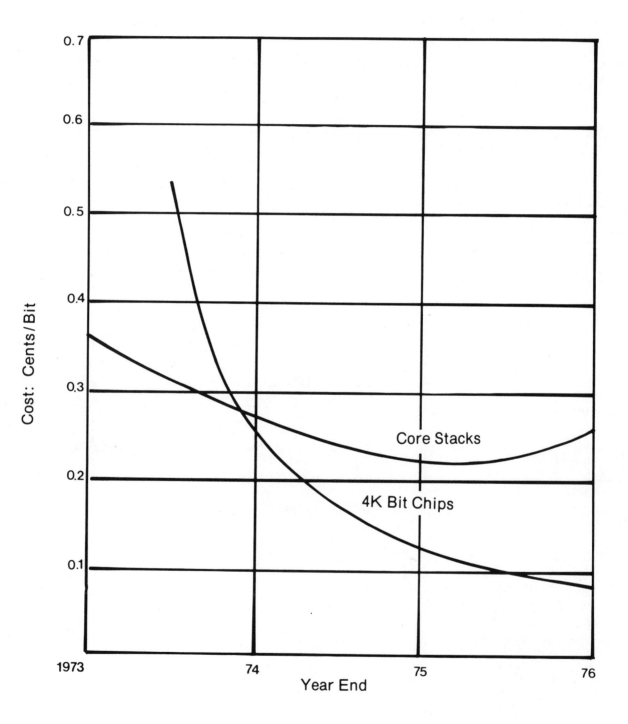

4.2 COMMUNICATIONS

It seems to be generally agreed that the cost of communications is dropping rapidly but not as rapidly as processor costs. This statement is, however, misleading. The fact that 50,000 telephone calls can be routed down a 1cm optical waveguide does not reduce communications costs until the technology is implemented by the PTTs and common carriers. Similarly a communications satellite cannot cheapen European circuits costs if the satellite is blown up on the launching pad.

At the present time, communications costs are going up, not down. Compared with the USA, it is going to take much longer for European organizations to benefit from digital networks, computer-based switching and public data networks. These new systems are going to take so long to develop that we would be surprised to see any cost reductions passed on to users until the late 1980s. Indeed, in the first half of the decade, tariffs could rise as the PTTs need to raise capital for the new networks.

Packet-switching might help some companies financially (perhaps on international connections) but, on the whole, the outlook is pessimistic.

4.3 CENTRAL SITE

The same developments in technology which will benefit the user of small processors will also help the user of mainframe systems. However, the improvements will not be anything like as great.

There are two major reasons for this. Firstly, for a mainframe supplier manufacturing costs are as little as 15% of the selling price of the system (12% for IBM). The rest is made up of marketing, administration, R & D and, of course, profit. Clearly, even a substantial fall in production costs will only have a marginal impact on the selling price. The second reason is that some mainframe suppliers (especially IBM) still do a large proportion of their business on a rental or lease basis. The effect of any large jump in cost/performance might cause the supplier to find a lot of obsolete hardware on his doorstep. IBM, for example, does regularly release slightly more powerful processors for slightly less money. But this must be seen against a background of ever increasing software complexity and size which serves well to soak up much of that capacity. In summary, the mainframe prices will reduce steadily (for equivalent power) but nothing too dramatic is likely to happen.

4.4 OVERALL EFFECT

Figure 14 attempts to assimilate these trends and to assess the impact on distributed system costs. For reasons of simplicity (in locating the minimum cost points), it is assumed that central site costs will remain the same. Obviously, the curves are only notional but they do seem to suggest that, for a given system, the minimum cost solution will be more distributed in 1990 than today.

Figure 14

Effects of Technology Trends on Distributed System Costs

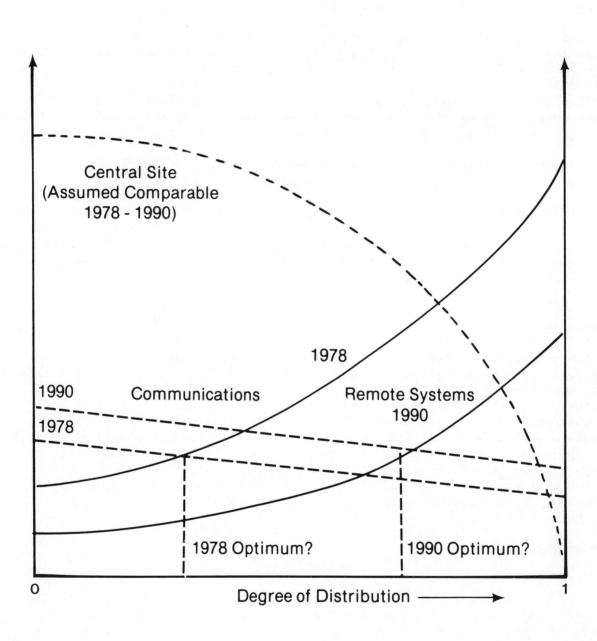

Central Site
(Assumed Comparable
1978 - 1990)

1978

1990

Communications

Remote Systems
1990

1978

1978 Optimum?

1990 Optimum?

0

Degree of Distribution ⟶

1

CHAPTER V

IMPLICATIONS FOR THE DP DEPARTMENT

"DP's success is measured in terms of the
proliferation of its capabilities throughout the
corporation and the ultimate loss of its own
identity as an independent corporate suborganization."
                Charles P. Lecht in his book 'The Waves of Change'.

Lecht's concept of the 'disappearing computer department' is one with
which there is much sympathy. Many companies making a major commitment to
DDP do have much diminished dp departments. But this has come about as a
conscious policy, not as an inevitable side effect of introducing
distributed processing.

What is certainly not happening is that users themselves are taking over
the jobs of designing and programming systems. We have only heard one
person express the view that this might be a good thing to happen. Who,
then, is doing the development work? In some cases, the dp department is
still doing it. As mentioned previously, many dp managers have been
pleasantly surprised at the ease with which systems can be developed (see
IR9 and IR6). On the other hand, some organizations have made good use of
systems houses and software houses (see IR1, IR8, and IR11).

The new role for the reduced computer department seems to be:

1. to lay down corporate guidelines and standards for the use of DDP

2. to work with users in the specification of their needs and in the
   design of an effective solution

3. the evaluation and acquisition of hardware and facilities

4. the selection of a software house to produce the application code
   and to monitor and control that activity

5. to assist and co-ordinate in the implementation phase

6. to provide ongoing program maintenance and support

This last point is particularly important. The use of an external software
house working on a fixed price contract helps to control development costs.
However, maintenance support by a software house does not seem to work
well. The installation of terminals and remote processors tends to
encourage users to think more about 'their' system and this usually
generates more change requests than with batch systems. To have a software
house deal with these changes on an as-and-when basis can prove expensive
(especially if the service company is unable to guarantee the availability
of a programmer familiar with the system).

An in-house team to support such maintenance activity has been found to be more effective. Two small qualifications are required; the team should include programmers who worked on the development of the original system (perhaps seconded to the software house) and users should be quoted a price to cover the cost of the change. This acts as a brake on the more frivolous amendments.

DP managers should budget for extensive training for their systems staff. This is especially so if they have only had batch experience; additional skills in the area of terminals, communications, transaction processing and minis may be required. Such expenditure on training is a good way of assuring the viability of new DDP systems.

The load on the operations department may well decrease, unless the batch load for non-DDP applications increases anyway. However, the operations department will need to undertake the important function of network management. This is considered further in the Technical Report (Volume 2).

CHAPTER VI

IMPLICATIONS FOR MANAGEMENT

"My company has had nothing but success
with distributed processing..."
        Dick Stoner
        Vice President, Administration
        Gulf Atlantic Distribution Services

In earlier sections of this report, we have tried to emphasize the need
to 'test' a variety of system solutions (each having a different degree of
distribution) in order to determine the optimum configuration for a given
application or set of applications. However, one aspect of DDP which
particularly interested the author at the beginning of this study was
whether the technique was better suited to certain corporate structures than
others. This issue was raised with a number of the specialists (and users)
interviewed and the general conclusion reached was that DDP seems to work
particularly well for the following types of organization:

- those which are 'naturally' decentralized
- conglomerates (or horizontally-integrated companies)
- project-oriented organizations
- geographically widespread concerns (e.g. multinationals)
- matrix-structured corporations

A good example of a 'naturally' decentralized organization is the J. C.
Penney Co. (IR7). The company operates as a number of self-contained,
geographically widespread units each of which has fairly autonomous
management.

Companies which are widely diversified, perhaps by acquisition, often
find it difficult to handle the large variety of application needs imposed
by the users. Two examples are the Vickers Group, (IR3) and the Tilling
Group, (IR5). Sometimes the problem is made even more acute by the
'inheritance' of dp systems in the new subsidiaries.

The construction industry is a good example of project-oriented
organizations. Not only do their data processing needs vary substantially
from time-to-time but the locations at which that computer power is required
also changes. Many such companies have adopted minicomputers as a
convenient means of providing such facilities as and where it is needed and
with a communications link (usually dialed) to some central mainframe
resource for large jobs such as PERT runs. Another example of this approach
is the use of minis on exploratory drilling platforms in the oil business.

Some corporations we spoke to are considering the 'divisionalization' of
their data processing activities. One company in the UK has, on their own
admission, made such a mess of their central dp service department that they
have asked user departments requesting new applications to find other ways
of doing it. A group has been set up in the dp department to advise users

on how to go about this and to provide practical help in finding hardware
and software suppliers. It is unfortunate that the company had to resort to
this radical action...good management has more to do with avoiding problems
than solving them. But it is interesting that the early user departments
(two who bought turnkey mini systems) have been so successful that users
still on the central mainframe are clamouring for release.

As explained in Chapter 2, the inordinately high cost of international
circuits makes distributed systems particularly suitable for multinational
corporations. Good examples of this are W. R. Grace Inc., (IR11) and
Atlantic Containers Ltd. (IR14).

Few dp professionals with even a passing interest in DDP can have failed
to read or hear about Citibank's massive commitment to the minicomputer
(IR1). What tends to get overlooked about developments at Citibank is major
restructuring of the organization which has taken place under the banner of
'Project Paradise'. Instead of the corporation being organized on
functional grounds (e.g., customer accounting, fund transfers, currency
dealing) it has now been restructured into customer service divisions. Each
of these 'banking groups' looks after a particluar type of customer, e.g.,
overseas customers, New York retail customers, multinationals, US
corporations. In order to provide a full range of customer services, each
of these groups needs to be able to perform all the functions previously
undertaken by most, if not all, of the 'old' divisions. This gives the bank
a 'matrix' structure and the use of minicomputers is intended to enable the
banking group to use special purpose interconnected systems to perform these
functions. Installation Report IR1 provides more information on this system.

Of course, there are still too few operational distributed systems for
me to produce statistical evidence for the claims made in this section. The
conclusions drawn are based upon very preliminary observations of some of
the major DDP networks already installed and tested against the views of
many informed specialists in the profession. The basic assertion is, to a
large extent, self evident; DDP is more suited and easier to cost justify
for some organizations than others. If a single company has a combination
of two or more of the attributes listed above, then the distribution
approach is even more relevant.

CHAPTER VII

PLANNING GUIDELINES

The following checklist of points is designed to highlight some of the major findings of this study. It also provides some management guidelines for the planning of distributed systems.

1. DDP is already a proven technique. Enough systems, and in adequate variety, have already been installed to justify this statement. Managers can feel safe about considering DDP solutions to user requirements and, if the distributed approach seems to be most cost/effective, they can also feel safe about giving the go-ahead (having considered some of the safeguards listed below).

2. Do not underestimate the impact DDP can have on corporate data processing activities. Indeed, if extensive use of the technique can be foreseen, then the whole dp strategy may need to be reviewed.

3. The effective involvement of user management and staff in the development of a distributed system can be crucial. Management is advised to review the way in which users are involved in system design and development activities. A program of education might help.

4. Plan well and budget well for the retraining of dp staff in anticipation of the development of a DDP network. Some or all of the following techniques and technology may be new; terminals, communications, transaction processing, minicomputers, microprocessors, networking and data bases.

5. Ensure that the dp department has access to a full inventory of skills and advice. This may be built up through training, acquisition of new staff and retention of consultants.

6. Make your first system a small pilot scheme (but one which is well-justified in its own right). Keep it simple! It is very tempting for technical staff to add facilities and end up by making the system too complex for a safe, assured project. The best 'complex' systems are based upon simple, easy-to-understand and easy-to-maintain components.

7. Moving away from a relatively 'safe' centralized mainframe system to a mini-based approach requires a firm management as well as technical commitment. Make sure you understand what you are letting yourself in for.

8. 'Packaged' systems and network architectures can ease implementation and provide a base for the long-term planning and development of system enhancement and extensions. However, care is required to ensure that the packaging does not constrain development by restricting flexibility and the ability to benefit on an ongoing basis from improvements in technology.

9. Always ensure that the new system has been conceived to meet well-defined organizational objectives and it is not merely a mechanism for 'patching up' the ills of an existing system.

10. In order to avoid the ever increasing maintenance burden, managers should ensure that their technical staff produce programs which are easy to maintain. Wherever possible, new systems should incorporate features which enable users to make minor changes to applications by themselves without the need for program changes.

11. As might be expected, there is an inverse relationship between the level of risk involved and the cost/benefit potential of any particular technique adopted. Of the main approaches described in this report the following are listed in order of risk (least risk first, most risky last):

- packaged DDP product
- small business computers
- network architecture
- minicomputer-based solution

On the other hand, the same approaches (listed in order of potential cost/benefit first, worst last) are:

- mini-computer based solution
- packaged DDP product
- small business computers
- network architectures

Again, this assertion is a generalization based upon a small sample; the reader must come to his own conclusions based upon the assessment of alternative solutions designed for his own organization.

12. Do not underestimate the likely impact on the central site. Although network architectures supplied by the mainframe companies are likely to increase the size of the central CPU, other approaches can dramatically reduce central-site processor requirements. The effects of such a reduction include:

- the use of a mini instead of a mainframe CPU

- the use of a bureau (corporate or public) instead of an 'in-house' machine

- the releasing of processor resources for new batch (or centralized teleprocessing applications)

- the postponing of a CPU upgrade

- the complete elimination of the central-site installation as we know it today

It has been suggested that if the mainframe survives DDP, then it will have more to do with the Data Processing Manager and corporate politics than the computer salesman. However, it was found during the course of this study that many DP Managers were unconcerned (if not quite pleased) about the degraded role of the central site.

13. Organizations committed wholly or partially to IBM will have a difficult time ahead of them. The DPD salesman will be selling him SNA for his distributed system and the GSD salesman will be trying to sell him a network of Series/1 minis. SNA is difficult to cost/justify and contrary to claims that will provide him with a sound base for his long-term communications planning, could impose many restrictions on the use of new public data networks and non-IBM terminal systems. SNA has a poor track record. On the other hand, the Series/1 offers a much more flexible and open-ended solution in return for greater implementation effort. The Series/1 at the time of writing, has no track record at all on distributed processing networks. This situation is confusing for the IBM customer (and for the DP salesman who is often reluctant to let the GSD salesman into his customer sites).

The present feeling of the author is that SNA may be a higher-risk long-term approach to DDP than the use of minis (although easier to implement in the short-term). There are no easy guidelines on this problem. Each situation needs to be assessed independently. However the following points may be of assistance:

- do not let IBM decide which approach is best for your company

- insist on seeing the Series/1 salesman and obtain information about that product as well as SNA products

- invest well in internal training and the use of well-informed external advice to help resolve the issue

- a small, self-contained pilot project using the Series/1 could improve the department's ability to make the decision (if time permits)

- the use of ITS or 3780/JES emulator could be an easy way of introducing Series/1 remote processors; more sophisticated networking techniques could then be gradually built on this

As time goes on, more DDP-related software will become available from a variety of sources for Series/1. This will ease implementation and make management decision making and planning easier. It is the author's opinion that DDP networks based upon the Series/1 will become more widespread (and successful) than those based upon SNA products.

In summary, the DDP is not merely a fad but represents a major change in the direction of corporate data processing strategies. Early operational systems have established the practicality of the concept. But great care is still required; the benefits are many, but so are the pitfalls.

APPENDIX A

This appendix contains three Supplementary Papers which are taken from Volume 2. These will serve to reinforce the information in the body of this report. The papers are:

SP1: Distributed Systems - An Attempt at a Definition

SP2: DDP: Anticipating the Future

SP3: Distributed Processing in Practice

<u>SUPPLEMENTARY PAPER NUMBER 1</u>

Subject Area: Concepts and Strategies

Title: <u>Distributed Systems: An Attempt at a</u>
          <u>Definition</u>

Source: Philip H. Dorn
          Dorn Computer Consultants Inc., USA

Transcript of presentation at Online
Conference on Distributed Systems

What am I going to do for you in this report: I am going to do a high wire act and if I fall off the wire, I am going to land in the mouths of the tigers. Let me try to define distributive data processing. Its a nice simple assignment, its a nice way to spend a few minutes. It is a mildly death defying act.

I will try to present some examples of systems with which I am reasonably familiar, systems that, for one reason or another, seem to be or do not seem to be distributed processing. Some of these thoughts are new and some are stolen from various dp pundits over the world. I am totally confused of course, but then I am allowed to be as I am a Consultant.

Back last May the Editor of Datamation, John Kirkley, posed three great questions for our time. I know that no-one ever reads the editorials in the magazines, but these were three significant questions which should have been answered a long time ago. First question is a traditional question: "How many angels can dance on the head of a pin?" Perhaps we should change that to how many circuits can dance on the head of a pin. Second question was: "Who invented peanut butter?" and the third question is "What is distributed data processing?" John categorized these as the three gret unanswered questions of our time. He suggested that research, which of course, means money, can solve these first two questions. In fact we already know the answer to question number two and this is an American answer. We are really convinced that Billy Carter invented peanut butter. The third question has really escaped any solution up-to-date except for a few crazy people like myself who keep trying to answer it. I am either brave or stupid - take your pick - but let me just dive in and answer this question of what is distributed data processing.

It is my answer alone. It does not fit the definition of any manufacturer (either mainframe or minicomputer). We see the term distributed data processing used in every type of publication. I suggest when you first see it, you step back and take a very hard look at what the author is really describing before you say "Ha, Ha! That is distributed data processing!" People use the term in a variety of different ways; different things for different people.

It is not networking - I am fairly sure of that. If I knew how to define networking I could be completely sure. As far as I can see I can make it in six points. Without all six points the system you are trying to describe could be a very great success of course, but it may not be distributed data processing. These are:

- Centralized management
- Centralized programming
- Remote users
- Remote processing hardware
- Communications (?)
- Remote operational database.

Let me plough back through 6 points and take them each in turn and we will see what systems fit and what systems do not fit.

Centralized management - we deal here with functional management, operational management if you will. Somebody has to be in charge of the functions one is trying to perform or the whole thing falls apart. Every remote site, 'node' if you will, has to be doing the same objectives. If you have that sort of situation, there has to be a boss in charge of everything. Establish the targets, make sure that they are met. Centralized management exists to ensure that the same targets are met in all places, to make sure that nobody gets off to solve ones own problems, to chase their own private goals.

The definition from the dictionary of the word 'distributed' uses the term 'dealt out', that implies that somebody actually dealt it out, passed out the responsibility. It does not imply, to my mind, that they sprang up from the grass all by themselves. If you have decentralization, you have a '1401 on every floor' syndrom, which is where I came into this industry 20 years ago. Many of us have worked at one point in our lives or another, in high rise office blocks where you find a 1401 on every floor except for the few guys who had installed Honeywell 200s. There has to be commonality of purpose, commonality of interests and someone has to sort out the politics. I do not want to push that one too far but it is there.

Centralized programming. To me this one is completely obvious - you have to do it. Apparently there are people who disagree with me. We are dealing fundamentally with 'remotes' that are doing the same thing, the onlky guarantee we have to get the job done right. We can get it done a lot of ways but to get it done right is to make sure it is done well by a single central group and centrally maintained to keep it all at same level. I do not want local programming capability in systems that I consider distributed processing systems. Frankly, there is a shortage of programmers in this world, how many programmers are there in the whole world? 200. There are a lot of people walking around who say they are programmers but it is the same 200 that we have always had. That is a fact of life and if any of you have studied large programming groups you know that in any group of 100 there are 3 or 4 that are really good, 15 to 20 that are comfortably acceptable, another small group that are mediocre but we let them get by because they are nice people or good looking girls. The other 50 are probably negative! In fact when you look at programmers on total scale of 100 points, the scale is really +50 to minus 50, you get down to that right hand side negative. So there is a shortage of real programmers in this world and if I have one I do not want him out there in a node, I want him up in the middle where I can get some work out of him that a lot of people can use.

There is not really a shortage of clerical people to enter orders or to trade commodities or to buy things. Sometimes we think there is a shortage, but not really. These are not programmer's machines. How do I prevent people out there from programming, very simple, I don't let them have compilers.

Remote users. Use real live users, people buying things and selling things and processing transactions, not data processing personnel. Real live users don't know anything about the machine, they do not care about it, they get paid for completing their functional tasks on time, within budget. Our job in data processing is to assist them in performing their tasks more effectively, more economically; nothing fancier than that. Now if you computer science people do not like what I say, I am sorry, I am not talking to computer science people. I very rarely do in fact. Computing is not (in a commercial world) an end in itself. It exists to serve the corporation or the institution; real live users, people who want to get the work done. You will notice I used the term efficiency? This is a business machine, an office machine. At 5 o'clock or 6 o'clock you turn off the key and go home. Two whole shifts of machine time are going down the drain. Isn't it dreadful! No, it's not terrible at all. You off the typewriter at 6 o'clock and go home, they turn off the dictating equipment, so they can turn off the computer also.

Remote processing hardware. The key word of course, is processing. I am not interested in systems which are based on dumb terminals. If you have a system with IBM 3270 terminals, you do not apply as a distributed system. Nor will you qualify if you have an intelligent terminal which has to be down line loaded. I want enough 'smart' to perform the functional tasks all the time whether the big machine is up or not. If I have to whistle down a telephone line and say 'please load my programs, I am ready to start working' you do not qualify. Curiously enough, most of the applications with which I have dealt, do not need a lot of computer. Processing speed is probably not a requirement. That is a general statement. I would like to have a machine which runs reasonably fast, but it seems to me to be more important that the machine be broad in the sense of being able to handle multiple peripherals, say 3 or 4 VDUs, a printer, some communications, control a 5 or 10 megabyte disk all at the same time, without seriously impeding the ability of the girls sitting at the displays scanning data. It does not take a lot of speed to stay up to that sort of thing. So it is a broad machine rather than a 'pointed' machine. I do not need a lot of processing power in this class of application, there is very little computing to be done to look at an inventory, subtract three and put the inventory back on the file. Its nice to have speed, it cannot hurt. All the minis are reasonably fast.

Communications. I said communications with a question mark. I will probably put three question marks after it. I am not yet ready to scrap a central facility and go to a completely peripheral network or a star type of network without a central machine. If I am going to have a central facility then I am going to want to talk to it very little (if I could) but I have to talk to it occasionally. Perhaps I would like to talk to it once a day to pick up the whole day's transactions at my place and ship them over there for all that night-time record keeping that central processors are very good at. I said communications and I am squirming on the point because I know of many areas in the world where distances are too long, communications costs are simply too expensive to be on-line all the time, you cannot do it in some places. For instance Australia is the classic case becuase you have really five cities sprawled across a land mass of 25,000 miles and the communications charges are extremely high to get say from Perth to Sydney. You would have to have a very very important application communications mode called the 727. Are you familiar with 727 mode? I suspect you are! It is rather amazing that one can take on an aeroplane and in a couple of hours its across the other side of the continent. It's much cheaper than communications lines and acceptable because it is a form of communication, something goes over and something comes back.

<u>Remote operational database</u>. Well this is the one that glues it all
together, it really controls the other five. A simple point; business be
kept and accessed at the local site where the work is being done. You can
do your file maintenance, that great big job of updating the files,
centrally; you can forward the results every night and have it ship to a
nice fresh file for you every morning but you had better have everything out
there at the node every day so that you can sell things and buy things.
Why? Because if you don't do it that way what are you going to do when the
big machine is down? Or the communications lines are down?

It seems to me that we are doing this whole exercise to provide local
functional capabilities. If we have to run for one, two or three days
without the central computer being available to update things, fine, no real
problem. It can get a little hairy with a small machine if you have been
trying to run for say 6/7 days because the chances are that your inventory
is now getting a little sloppy and your disk is getting a little bit full
with transactions and audit trails. You would like to clean it out every
nignt but if it takes every second or third night it does not matter.
Should you update 'on the fly' in the small machine out at the node, you can
argue this one both ways. I do not particularly think it necessary; after
all we have been running warehokuses and distribution points for years with
manual inventories which are only accurate once a year! So if we are a day
out on balance the world is not going to come to an end.

Nothing terribly dramatic about these 6 points. They seem to me that,
taken together, they really define what I consider to be distributed
processing.

Supplementary Paper Number 2

Subject Area: Concepts and Strategies

Title: <u>Distributed Systems: Anticipating the Future</u>

Source: Iann Barron

Paper presented at Online Conference
on Distributed Systems

Introduction

Judged by the number of conferences and the level of interest, there can be no doubt that distributed processing is fashionable. The question that needs to be asked is whether distributed processing is anything other than a fashion. It is this question that we want to explore, largely in a non-technical way. Firstly by asking what distributed processing means in terms of the computer products that will be available, then by considering what effect distributed processing has on the principles of computing, and finally by examining the application of distributed processing.

For the purpose of this discussion, a distributed system is a set of autonomous, but interacting, computers. The interesting thing is that there are three quite separate reasons why systems of this sort have become important:

- the advances in semiconductor technology are reducing the cost of processing and this means that it is becoming practicable to use a large number of processors in a system. Thus, the user who, in the past, required a large central processor has now to consider the alternative of using many smaller computers organized into a co-operating system.

- the greater understanding of the problems of software and system design has led to the concept of structured systems, so that the system is partitioned into distinct parts which intercommunicate by formal interfaces. This approach has obvious affinities to distributed processing, and a distributed system can form a good discipline for ensuring a structured approach.

- as the number of computers grows, so the opportunity for direct computer to computer communication increases. Thus, when computers were first used in business, bank transactions were entirely paper oriented, the company computer providing output for cheque preparation, which in turn ultimately provided input information to a bank computer. More recently, a system has been introduced whereby the transaction can be made by the transfer of magnetic tapes, so eliminating an intermediate stage of paper input/output. By the time that the majority of companies have computer-based accounts, there would be obvious advantages to the further step of direct computer to computer debiting.

It is extremely fortunate that the basic developments in hardware and software should be operating in the same direction as a perceived need from the users, and this must give added momentum to the development of distributed processing.

Just as there are three motivations behind the move to distributed processing, so the advocates of distributed processing claim three quite separate advantages for the appoach:

- that the cost of computing can be cut dramatically by using large number of small computers in place of a large computer.

- that the design and development of a system can be greatly
  simplified, while awkward problems like operating systems are
  eliminated.

- that distributed systems mirror more accurately the structure of
  real life applications, and so in some way are more natural.

We will argue that each of these claims is grossly overinflated, and
that the excessive claims made on behalf of distributed processing are a
positive disservice. At this level, distributed processing is another
technique to be added to the computer professionals' armoury, comparable to
interactive computing, which has value in specific areas, but also brings
its own disadvantages. However, underlying distributed processing is a more
fundamental concept, that of parallel computation, and in the long term it
is this theoretical concept which will change many of our ideas about
computing.

Distributed systems cost less

The pattern of distributed processing will be determined to a large
extent by the facilities provided by the computer manufacturer, so the point
of departure must be to ask how the concept of distributed processing will
be interpreted in future computer systems.

The most noticeable development in computing has been the improvement in
processor technology. The processor capability which cost $500,000 in 1955
can be purchased today for $300 and can be expected to cost $5.00 in 1980.
At the same time, the throughput of this capability has increased, perhaps
by a factor of 40 since 1955, with the likelihood of a further 2.5 times
enhancement by 1980. This means that raw processing capability, measured in
terms of, say, multiplications per unit processing cost, has increased by a
factor of 100,000 in twenty years, with the possibility of a further factor
of 100 in the next five years.

The most noticeable non-development in computing is that the improvement
in processing capability has not been passed on to the user in any direct
way. A certain manufacturer has been running an advertisement which claims
that the cost of performing a multiplication has fallen by a factor of
almost exactly 100 since 1955; the advertisement does not say that this
reduction has been achieved almost entirely by performance improvements, and
not by a reduction in the capital cost of the computer. It is all too easy
to be cynical about this situation, but there is a rationale which must be
remembered when considering future trends:

- the obvious point is that processing is only a small component of
  computing, so that reducing its cost does not necessarily reduce
  the cost of the computer. This can usually be thought of as for
  independant components - processing, information storage, access
  facilities and systems design. It is difficult to generalize,
  because of the wide variation between applications, but in most
  cases the true processing costs will be the least of four
  components. The situation is somewhat confused by the fact that
  the user does not see the true cost; for convenience it is loaded
  with miscellaneous system costs like standard software,
  installation, warranty, etc., so that it appears as a larger item
  in the bill than would otherwise be the case.

64

- from the customer's point of view, rather different factors are
  operating. The potential range of applications within a company
  for a computer are enormous; they are limited only by the cost of
  computing, the rate of change that is acceptable and the knowhow
  to apply the computer. As a result, if it is economic to install
  a computer costing $2,000,000, it is almost certainly worthwhile
  to spend even larger sums as the cost of the computer falls, in
  order to tackle the much wider range of problems that become
  economic. Add to this the natural tendency for humans to create
  empires, and it will become clear that established users will look
  for increased capability rather than reduced capital cost.

- finally, the manufacturer has little incentive to reduce the
  capital price of his product. For the mainframe manufacturer, at
  least, the market is inelastic. Organizations with the revenues
  to purchase larger computers are well defined and the market is
  penetrated; to reduce price would, therefore, reduce revenues.
  The minicomputer market appears to have a higher degree of
  elasticity, and there has been a slow decline in purchase price,
  but this must be managed carefully if the manufacturer is still to
  achieve an overall increase in revenues.

Thus a reasonable view of the market mechanisms is that the
manufacturers will operate to protect their revenues by offering the
existing market improved products with greater capability. The advantages
of reduced cost of processing are offered to a new sector of the market,
packaged as a rather different set of facilities. It is this pattern of
market stability which led to the development of the minicomputer as a
separate product and which is now creating a new marketplace for the
microcomputer. At this stage the microcomputer marketplace would appear to
offer a considerable degree of elasticity, and it will be interesting to see
how the revenues of the semiconductor survive the tenfold reduction in price
that will be possible with the introduction of single chip microprocessors
to replace current multichip systems. A reasonable projection is that the
manufacturers will be able to absorb the price reduction over a period of
three years and still maintain adequate revenue growth. However, it is
unlikely that such a quantum jump could be achieved again in the future.
The next question is to ask how products will be improved. For a mainframe
manufacturer, a distributed system must consist of a large computer
surrounded by a very large number of terminals, with differing degrees of
intelligence. This marketing emphasis will be to sell terminals and the
central system will be regarded as an inviolate whole.

The position of the minicomputer manufacurer is more complicated. At
present, his market comprises two distinct sectors - single sales of
commercial and scientific systems to end users and OEM volume sales of basic
hardware. The OEM sector is threatened because in the next three years the
microcomputer will achieve the logical complexity and performance necessary
to replace the minicomputer completely. The minicomputer manufacturer has a
choice, therefore, either to enter into direct competition, making his own
semiconductor products, or to move up market and to attempt to take a larger
share of commercial sales.

Currently, minicomputer companies like DEC, have an opportunity in the microcomputer market. They are in a strong cash position, and the entry costs are not excessive. Also, with their current minicomputer architecture and software they will have an edge in the emergent 16 bit microcomputer market which would be difficult for the semiconductor manufacturers to match. This situation will not last long, because early established products are likely to establish market dominance, and if the computer companies do not enter the market within the next year or so, the opportunity will be lost irretrievably. The alternative choice for the minicomputer manufacturer is to move up market. In part this can be done by offering more powerful systems created as distributed networks of computers – minicomputers, together with upgraded versions of existing products, and this must be the main marketing thrust for minicomputer companies. This approach does not, however, solve the basic problem of selling in the commercial market, which is to provide a higher level of support and software than is currently available. Until this is done the minicomputer will not be fully competitive in the commercial market. To do this will be expensive, and coupled with the reduction in volume as a result of losing the OEM market, it will reduce the price differential between the minicomputer and the mainframe. Both of these strategies for the minicomputer require considerable resources and will only be practicable for the largest companies; the others are likely to continue to retreat into the specialized system business. On the basis of their current activities, it might be expected that Data General will concentrate on the microcomputer market, while DEC attempts to pursue both strategies.

There is one option which has not been discussed. That is to build a computer as a network of microcomputers. Such an approach has obvious technical interest, and there are already some examples on offer. The Micral A from R2E provides a primitive system of this type, with up to eight Intel 8080 microprocessors connected to a common store. A more dubious example is the IMS hypercube. In this system, microcomputer units are interconnected on a four dimensional rectangular grid, so that each unit is connected to eight neighbours; three versions are being offered, the hypercube 1 with 16 units, the hypercube 2 with 81, the hypercube 3 with 256. Each unit consists of two Intel 8080 microprocessors, one to administer the intercommunication with other units, and one to perform useful work. While there are a few specialized applications, such as in radar data processing, where such systems can be used, they are not relevant to most applications, because we do not have the knowhow to partition problems in the requisite manner, nor are the software and operating system concepts yet available to make such systems readily usable.

The microprocessor itself is at present in a state of rapid change. Early microprocessors were extremely inconvenient to program, and required considerable electronic expertise to assemble into usable systems. The need to cut the cost of developing programs for microcomputers, and the development of single chip microcomputers will lead to a situation where the microcomputer has better software facilities than current minicomputers, and can be interconnected like meccano, without the need for any technical knowledge. Even so, the microcomputer will not be a suitable product for the end user; the cost of surrounding a microcomputer by the facilities necessary to make a useful system would be too high. Instead, microcomputer based products will be widely available and these may replace conventional and minicomputers in certain classes of application. A typical product of this might be a football ticket booking system, like that currently available on the GEC2050. It is to be expected that such products will be developed by companies with the necessary application knowledge and marketing ability rather than by general electronics companies or software houses. It is also unlikely that the semiconductor manufacturers attempt to offer a replacement for the general purpose minicomputer in the end user market; excluding OEM sales, minicomputer sales run at around 10,000 a year of which the semiconductor content of such systems will be negligible, so there would be little direct benefit to the semiconductor manufacturers in comparison to the investment involved.

Thus, although the decrease in raw processing costs will continue at least at the present rate over the next five years, there is no reason to expect that the development of minicomputers, or the increased use of distributed processing will alter the current pattern in established markets of stable prices and slowly improving cost performance capability.

Distributed sytems are easy to develop

The operating system in a centralized computer usually occupies a large part of the resident store and uses a considerable proportion of the processor time. Since a large part of most operating systems is concerned with scheduling and managing a multiprogramming regime, it might be thought that much of the operating system could be done away with in a distributed system. In fact, the opposite is the case, the operating system for a distributed computer has a more difficult task to perform and may be even larger in total.

At the level of the operating system the difference between centralized and distributed processing is comparable to the difference between time domain switching and space domain switching in a telephone system: in one case it is necessary to allocate resources in space. The allocation problem, which is a prime function of the operating system remains largely unchanged. In practice, a distributed operating system will be more complex for the following reasons:

- the use of a single processor to execute both the operating system and user tasks provides an automatic synchronization mechanism, since the use of non-interruptable code in parts of the operating system guarantees that the state of user programs and other parts of the operating system remain unchanged. This technique is almost invariably used when scheduling and adjusting system tables and it enables considerable simplification of the operating system.

- in a distributed system, the allocation of resources is more constrained because it is necessary to consider not only the availability of resources but also the band width of access to a resource. Thus, a disc filing system has a constant band width in a centralized system, but in a distributed system it has a variable band width determined by the communication path to the filing system.

- intercommunication between processes is likely to be greater so that there is a need for this part of the operating system to be more efficient; and yet the difficulty of intercommunication is increased because of the limited bandwidth and the synchronization problems.

It might be thought that these disadvantages would be offset to some extent by simplifications to the operating system made possible by the reduced cost of processing. It should not be essential to achieve the maximum utilization of the processor or storage, since these are no longer the high cost elements of the system. While this is true, the argument applies with equal force to a centralized system.

Operating systems are often criticized because they are too large, and detract from the ability of a computer to run user programs. This is a very partial view, because the operating system is providing services to user programs, which would otherwise have to be provided as part of the user program and so it makes the user programs smaller and easier to develop. Rather than reduce the size, there is every incentive to increase the size of the operating system so that more aspects of a program can be performed automatically. Thus the fact that the operating system for a decentralized computer is likely to be large should not be regarded as a criticism, but merely as a recognition that the programmer is provided with additional facilities.

Two further arguments may be put forward in favour of distributed processing and within reason, both of these can be accepted:

- the first argument is that a distributed system can be developed on a phased basis, so that the development can be spread across a large period and adapted to the experience of the earlier phases. This is certainly true and can be useful. Nevertheless, this does not obviate the need to plan the system from the start, and envisage the potential scope and requirements. At least equally is the ability to install a system on a phased basis and minimize the risk and capital investment at any time.

- the other argument is that a distributed system enforces good system design, because the existence of narrow interfaces between computers forces the programmer to partition his problem rigorously and to establish formal interface mechanisms. Such a discipline is extremely important, particulary for large systems and may be one of the most valuable side effects of distributed processing.

There is, therefore, some force to the argument that distributed processing will make systems easier to develop, but this arises more from the psychology of programmers and the realities of installation than from and fundamental characteristic of distributed processing.

Distributed processing is more natural

Most of the uses of the computers are inherently distributed. Company organizations are distributed with information and decision making being located at many points. Equally, most industrial systems are distributed, with multiple control points which interact to a limited extent. To conceive of a system in distributed terms is clearly extremely valuable: the question is whether it is necessary to realize this conception in a physically distributed form, or whether it could not be implemented equally well as a virtual distributed system - that is a set of interacting processors interacting in a centralized system. Since, in those terms, there is no conceptual difference between a centralized and distributed system, the choice becomes one of economics and security. There may be economic advantages in centralized parts of a system. The obvious example is file storage, because there are substantial economies of scale so one central file store is likely to cost much less than several smaller file stores which are distributed. Whether such centralization is justified will depend on the cost of storage and the cost of providing the required band width for remote access, i.e. the decision is essentially pragmatic. There may also be economic advantages of a practical nature in centralization, like centralized servicing or administration. To offset these potential advantages for centralization, distributed processing provides a natural mechanism of the concepts of security, enabling the possibility of recovery when parts of the system are unreliable.

Thus, while there may be considerable advantages to using a distributed model to represent accurately the overall properties of a system, the way in which this representation is mapped into a physical realization can be based on the quite different considerations of cost and reliability. It is this new freedom that the user will have to describe his system in one distributed form, but to implement it in another that will prove to be the significant advance.

SUPPLEMENTARY PAPER NUMBER 3

Subject Area: Concepts and Strategies

Title: Distributed Processing in Practice

Source: G. E. Cox & Partners Ltd. (with Diebold
         Europe at the time of writing)

Paper presented to Online
Conference on Distributed Systems

The Diebold Research Program-Europe, founded 12 years ago is an international co-opertive venture sponsored by over 120 leading commercial and governmental organizations in 18 different countries. Its purpose is to provide these organizations with the best obtainable information on which to base plans for developing information processing systems.

In the latter part of 1975, the Research Program investigated the current state of distributed processing in the business world in preparation for a research report. This paper outlines some of the findings.

The methodology which was employed consisted of collecting case studies from users, submitting questionnaires on distributed processing to various hardware manufacturers, interviewing communication specialists at the corporate headquarters of several major manufactures, and conducting a literature survey seeking information on distributed processing.

The emphasis of the investigations was on distributed processing the environment of large organizations where processing is first of all business oriented, then secondly of a general purpose nature. Ideally, we were searching for a corporate teleprocessing network, either with remote job entry or on-line processing, which, under the better principles of project management, converted to a global distributed processing scheme.

It is our feeling within the Research Program, here at the mid-point of the 1970's, that distributed processing will indeed be the automation vehicle of the 1980's.

Soon, we shall dismiss from our minds the question of whether distributed processing will predominate in the business automation world. Rather, we will be asking what options are available in this new way to process, when will it be economically feasible and how much effort will be required for conversion. The arguments of economy of scale which has supported centralized ADP organizations since the advent of data processing in the business world some twenty years ago are weaker today than ever before. This fact is generally not recognized but new concepts based upon technological advances must traditionally fight their way to acceptance by promises of superior performance under off-set costs. Distributed processing will bring a wide repertoire of cost-performance arguments to establish its due place in the data processing field, while providing superior performance in many application areas.

No author, no manufacturer, no user has been successful in putting forth an industry-wide accepted definition of distributed processing. The Diebold Research Program was faced with this roadblock in its investigations, but by analysing the case studies which were said to be distributed processing, by manufacturer and user alike, three criteria were deduced. These three crtiteria provide flexibility in developing the concept, yet are quite definitive.

The first criterion is that the computing system possess two or more geographically displaced processors or CPUs. These processors moreover, must be application logic oriented. That is, application programs, or portions of programs, are loaded and run on these processors.

The second criterion is that the two or more displaced processors be "linked".

This linkage is accomplished through telecommunications, perhaps with data buffering at various points, which in effect establishes a processor-to-processor link. Much debate ensues among our staff whether to include tape-swapping, that is that trading of magnetic tapes between computers, as legitimate distributed processing linkage. Finally, we did decide to include this type of linkage, although recognizing that its technological prognosis for the future is indeed not encouraging. It is well to note at this point that teleprocessing linkage is the most critical aspect in systems engineering for distributed processing, requiring considerable attention from both management and system designers, The major system parameters of reliability, performance, cost and security must be integrated into the linkage, or what we call the network topological architecture.

The third and last criterion for distributed processing is that the network created by the two or more displaced, linked processors be confined within an organizational boundary.

In other words, the network is dedicated to a corporation or an institution - it possesses corporate "stand alone" capability. This criterion sets distributed processing apart from what are commonly called computer networks. A computer network confined within one organization is distributed processing: however, if the computer network is a federated computing endeavour between several organizations, then, of course, it does not qualify as distributed processing.

Perhaps it would be instructive to quickly state which suspect configurations are not distributed processing.

Remote job entry is not distributed processing, because application logic is not loadable or resident at the terminal. Non-integrated systems, supported by dispersed stand-alone computers in a corporation, do not lead to distributed processing because the linkage is missing. The ARPA network in the United States is not distributed processing, although often cited as such, because the network is not confined to one organization - it serves a federation of universities for computer resource sharing. Time-sharing may participate in a distributed processing scheme, but does not define it in light of the third criterion.

Distributed processing does not necessarily imply the decentralization of the ADP function in an organization. It may be a popular misconception that it always does. This misconception has arisen due to a thoroughly indoctrinated sense of what data processing has meant - that computers must be supported by specialized ADP personnel, operators, programmers and system analysts, who cannot be restrained from developing new systems or changing old ones. While the latter probaly true, the former is not.

No case study on distributed processing was discovered either in Europe or North America, whose objective was the decentralization of the ADP function.

We are cognizant, however, of several instances where feasibility studies on decentralization using distributed processing are in progress. This fact, the divorce of distributed processing from decentralization borne out by the investigation, may seem puzzling.

The key to the puzzle, and the explanation why distributed processing system can continue centralized ADP policies, lies in the administration of the remote intelligence. First of all we have found in the advanced case studies a lack of the usual ADP personnel at the remote sites. That is, the operators, programmers and system analysts. Second, the compliers at the remote computing sites were turned off, not in use, or non-existent. Well, who mans those remote computers, you may ask ? Actually one of two procedures are used: either the application logic, that is, the application programs, are pre-linked into the remote computing device by corporate ADP personnel as an in-house turn-key system or the application logic is remotely loaded over the network communication lines. The latter case is called down-line loading and is prerequisite to unattended operations in general-purpose distributive computing.

Let me give you an illustration how it can work. Users at branch "X" in Amsterdam operate an accounts payable system in real-time, using a minicomputer. At night summary results are transmitted over the leased lines to the corporate centre in The Hague for corporate MIS processing and permanent storage. This system continues to be maintained by the corporate centre, as in the past, under batch processing. When a systems change has been completed by the business systems department and tested on the corporate mainframe, the updates program module is transmitted over the same leased lines to branch "X" in Amsterdam and automatically loaded into the resident job library with an accompanying message to the system user on the ramifications of the change. Turn-key maintenance and unattended operations allow the advantages of centralized ADP systems development to be combined with the advantages of stand-alone processing capabilities in a distributed processing scheme.

In summary on this point, I would like to remark that decentralized processing will be an exception rather than the rule. The rule, well established, will remain: centralized corporate systems engineering.

Now I would like to turn our attention to the basic equipment configurations of distributed processing. This categorization was devised early in the DRP investigations to assist in the evaluations of case studies.

The first configuration is tape swapping which was mentioned earlier. This has been a common practice in a considerable number of companies, even before the term distributed processing appeared on the ADP scene, so I will not spend time on this technique.

The second configuration is what we have labelled "local editing". Local editing is characterized by intelligent terminals, which are data entry and display devices, possessing a limited capacity for stand-alone processing. Usually, the local editing configuration supports an inter-departmental type of distributed processing as opposed to, say, an inter-divisional/regional type. For example, local editing can be found in a factory operating with a small mainframe.

Local editing will play a dominant role in data processing in the future as far as the eye can see. We in the Research Program can conceive of no substitute for it in a wide application range, and I would like to explain why. First of all, batch processing for operational systems will sink into disuse in the next ten years, replaced by real-time processing. Along with this decline of batch and corresponding rise of real-time processing, we shall see, and many of you will effect, the elimination of centralized data entry, that is, batch keypunching. Keypunching will all but disappear, because real-time systems require a different rhythm of input - in fact - demand input. Data entry at the sites of the real-time terminals. A simple exercise then in cost-effectiveness principles will show, in order to conserve communications resources, that: (1) user data input should be buffered and (2) data input should be locally edited for corrections, completeness and sequence. Since intelligence is required for these activities, it costs marginally more to application-process this locally edited data, for example, to print out a work order or purchase order. Please allow me to review your principal alternatives to local editing: either batch keypunching and processing are retained: or centralized keypunching is retained for a real-time system; or each non-intelligent terminal communicates continually with the network host. For these reasons, we say that local editing has a long future. Examples of local editing proliferate. I find it impossible not to be confronted with one when I read the weekly trade journals.

Remote batch is another unique configuration of distributed processing, almost solely found in a corporate inter-divisional/regional environment. Here, a corporate mainframe communicates with a remote minicomputer. On line, the minicomputer functions as a remote-job-entry-like terminal. Off-line, the mini is a stand-alone computing device. In the Research Program we are defining remote batch as the interrogation of remote files or data bases for local batch processing, most probably at the corporate mainframe site. In this configuration of distributed processing, the advantages of remote job entry are combined with the advantages of stand-alone computing in a powerful cost-effective way. Again, through case studies, we have discovered why. The remote minicomputer can be operated either in the batch mode, in-line, or in real-time. The batch mode usually means local ADP support. In-line, transaction processing is interesting when the minicomputer processes some data off-line, otherwise only the store-and-forward buffering capabilities of the mini are called into use and this may be wasteful. But it is the off-line use of the minicomputer as the base for a real-time system which provides overpowering cost advantages coupled with improved system reliability. The network host mainframe may continue to operate in the batch mode for MIS systems, with linear output, requiring large sorts and merges, while the remote minicomputer drives a local real-time operational system. The real-time requirement is saved the high communication costs, being buffered from the operating complexities and often uncontrollable load conditions of the central mainframe. In this way, distributed processing is an effective catalyst in converting from batch processing in the remote job entry mode to local real-time processing.

One of the best case studies of remote batch distributed processing to our knowledge is at the Prudential Insurance Company of America, corporate-based in New Jersey. There, minicomputers are employed at regional centres to provide local interactive processing on insurance claims and accounting systems while maintaining corporate data banks via leased lines linkage at night. This distributed processing network extends across the continental United States, from New York to Los Angeles. At night, however, something very unique happens. Input for a variety of common regional batch systems is transmitted to the corporate centre for processing. The corporate centre in turn assigns and transmits the nationally combined data to specific regional minicomputers for application batch processing. For example, the minicomputer at one regional centre performs the financial commission system processing for the complete network each night; another regional centre performs the sales commission processing for the complete network; and so forth. After processing, the results are re-routed via the corporate centre to the respective regional centres. In addition to the leased lines, dial-up communications are possible between the regional centres, thereby increasing the reliability of the network by several orders of magnitude. Also the provision has been planned where regional minicomputers use local time-sharing services to enhance computing power. Maximum flexibility, cost-effectiveness and improved reliability are the trademarks of this system. We noted, moreover, that all system design and maintenance are performed by corporate ADP staff personnel on a turn-key basis. Remote batch distributed processing is indeed powerful and possible as this case study bears out.

The next configuration of distributed processing is what we have labelled "hierarchical data base". It is characterized by dispersed computing devices operating data base management systems. These data bases communicate, interactively, with one another per programmed instructions built into the network operating system or by application program override commands. The primary objective of this configuration is to maintain functionally structured data for realtime processing which is globally consistent. In other words, the geographically dispersed and structured data bases "resonate" with a very minimum of data inconsistencies. One may question and rightly so, whether such a demand on the network design is unnecessarily extravagant. After all, using the remote batch mode, the data bases may be mutually updated by night-time processing. The answer to this may come from another question: how are large multi-processing backup installations justified? To both questions, the same answer: the corporation has an exceedingly high requirement for operating reliability and corporate controlled data storage, and in some instances, corporate staff manipulation of operational field data. The advantages which distributed processing brings over duplex, backup are (1) better reliability of processing through the parity of data at several locations combined with stand-alone hierarchical processing and (2) better availability of computing power for remote real-time processing.

Computer networks is the last configuration of distributed processing to be investigated here. This configuration boasts of geographically dispersed corporate computers, mostly mainframes, which communicate constantly with one another under the control of a very sophisticated network operating system which includes the capabilities of remote batch and hierarchical data base processing. In simplistic terms, the objective of the network is to make all the computing resources and stored data available to users while keeping the facilities transparent. Only when desired, does the user specify by program commands which resources are to be assigned to a particular job. Such a configuration provides the ultimate in back-up and reliability while providing efficient use of resources.

Capabilities of Network Operating System

- File Sharing
- Device Sharing
- Program Sharing
- Program Data Sharing
- Bootstrapping

Before we proceed to the state-of-the-art in 1975, several explanations on the major capabilities of an ideal network operating system may throw additional light on the objectives of distributed processing. In the DRP investigations, five major capabilities have been recognized, although only the computer network configuration may possess all five. The first capability is file sharing. This means that a remote processor is able to access a local file or data base. The second capability is device sharing. Here, for example, a utility sort and merge program and necessary disk devices are available to remote minicomputers in the network. The third capability is program sharing. Through this capability on-line, turn-key maintenance can be effected. From the mainframe host, programs can be lined into remote core. The fourth capability is program data sharing, which provides for the interactive exchange of data between two or more remote processors. The hierarchical data base configuration would be based solely upon this capability. The fifth and last capability of an ideal network operating system is called bootstrapping. Bootstrapping allows the host mainframe, for example, to load and execute a program at a remote computer site. When one considers these five capabilities carefully, the realization comes that operators and programmers, perhaps even system analysts, may be unnecessary at the remote operational nodes in the distributed processing network.

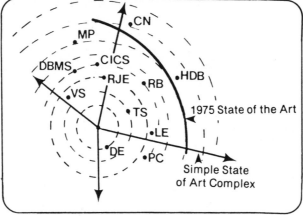

Now to that state-of-the-art. Please keep in mind that what is being presented here is oriented to computing in large corporations and institutions. This diagram which you see indicates two things: first, the degree of the relative complexity of the basic configurations of distributed processing as compared against typical large mainframe system configurations. For example, in the upper left sector, going from the comparatively simpler systems at the centre outwards to the more complex systems, we see: virtual storage, remote job entry, CICs, DBMs, and multi-processing. This sector represents the centralized processing, mainframe reliant, operating philosophy. The middle sectors represent, of course, distributed processing. From the centre one sees TS, which is tape-swapping; LE, local editing; RB, remote batch; HDB, hierarchical data base; and CN, computer network. In the lower-most sector, we may observe specialized systems, such as data entry and process control.

The second purpose of the graph is to report the state-of-the-art in 1975. The crux of the matter is that the hierarchical data base and computer network appear to be beyond the grasp of even larger ADP users.

Immediately, one suspects the lack of "off-the-shelf" technology as the reason why these two configurations of distributed processing have yet to find user acceptance. Partly, this is true. There is, however, another reason which is more revealing. In the approximately twenty case studies across an industry spectrum, one common factor was easily recognized: design ingenuity provided the basis for the implementation of distributed processing. The impetus for implementation did not spring from strategic executive directives. What happened was that one or two DP personnel found a progressive and cost-savings approach to an old operational system problem by using distributed processing. Cost justification of the scheme was more or less relegated to a formality.

Design ingenuity has, consequently, led to the prevalence of distributed processing which is constrained to well-defined application tasks. But design ingenuity is an impossible prerequisite for unconstrained, general purpose computing. Now how do these conclusions apply to the fact that the hierarchical data base and computer network configurations are excluded from the 1975 state-of-the-art? The answer is that these configurations are general purpose solutions - they are too expensive to implement as dedicated solutions for localized systems. Such dedicated distributed processing needs will opt for the local editing and remote batch configurations, rather than for the hierarchical data base or computer network because they are more cost-effective.

We will not wait long before we may observe the hierarchical data base and computer network configurations in operation. Several large companies have initiated feasibility studies in this direction. Furthermore, several medium size corporations are in the first phases of implementation. 1976 and 1977 will witness the documentation and publication of these pioneering steps towards distributed processing.

In the DRP investigations, the primary rules of thumb for the local editing and remote batch configurations are: (1) to keep volatile data at the source; and (2) to cover remote operational systems with autonomous intelligence. For the hierarchical data base and computer network configurations, the rule of thumb will be: limit the corporate computer to DP staff functions, like systems development, mass storage and back-up.

I have mentioned design ingenuity as the common factor having been the impetus for distributed processing to date. In this context, it would be instructive to review some of the "reasons" for implementing distributed processing.

In the broadcasting industry, two cases have offered an identical reason: to integrate local process control minis with the corporate general-purpose network.

In hospital administration, the reason is very curious: to provide centralized administration. In this case study which we believe will be quite common in the next several years, distributed processing leads to centralization. This is a good counter-example to the DP manager who professes that distributed processing in synonymous with a plan of decentralization.

In one large credit institution, the justification was to reduce transactional turnaround time, thereby increasing corporate profitability. This reason, to speed up the flow of transactions over large distances, will be common in the banking industry in future when justifying distributed processing.

One heavy manufacturing concern did not quite succeed in ADP centralization, with the result that a number of factories retained their mainframes. Now the introduction of RJE type linkage among these mainframes is providing a configuration which we have labelled distributed processing by default - that is, default on centralization. It is quite ironic that users who considered themselves behind the times with their scattered mainframes, suddenly through telecommunication linkage, feel quite avant garde.

You notice, of course, what is missing: the executive objective to provide general purpose corporate computing in a cost-effective and reliable way which promises to provide greater user autonomy and consequently satisfaction. Such an objective can only spring from corporate feasibility studies which have just begun to be intiated in the business world.

To summarize the benefits we can say from our investigations that distributed processing will give better operational control in product-oriented tasks; that it can be utilized to augment mainframe capabilities by providing localized real-time processing; that distributed processing will lower costs in a teleprocessing network; and that it will promote incremental growth patterns of hard and software acquisition.

The forfeitures of distributed processing are, strangely enough, more speculative than the possible wins. Security is certainly a valid issue. But which aspects of security are called into question: wire-tapping? A survey conducted by the Research Program among seven manufacturers revealed that they were also perplexed on this issue. How can one operate a "closed DP shop" with distributed processing ? The other possible major forfeiture of distributed processing over, say, remote job entry is in the area of uniformity - uniformity of systems development, of cost accounting, of personnel recruitment, or hardware acquisition etc. Of course, this is only a problem when ADP personnel are decentralized along with the distribution of computer intelligence. We have mentioned that this is the rare case. These problems will not be resolved by computer technological breakthroughs. We have mentioned that this is the rare case. These problems will not be resolved by computer technological breakthroughs. They are traditional management problems. Management itself, in some instances, will be the effective brake on the industry swing to distributed processing, because of the scale of effort involved with establishing new policy procedures relating to the distributed processing profile.

How will distributed processing evolve in the 1980's? We may safely speculate that hardware acquisition will not be a major deterrent to distributed processing. Rather, the point of contention will lie in the economics of network management and the ADP organization. The Diebold Research Program – Europe discerns two trends of paramount importance. These two evolutionary paths of equipment development and system software support represent the respective vendors' marketing strategies.

It remains to be seen whether an acceptable degree of compatibility will emerge between these two approches to distributed processing.

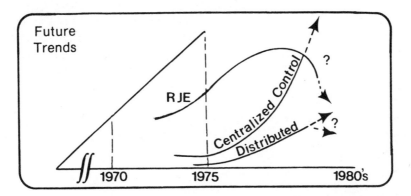

The first path of evolution we have labelled "centralized control". Here, the retained and upgraded mainframe or mainframes at the corporate data-processing will exert network operating control. This type of DP organization will be supported by the star network topology with the corporate ADP department at the centre of the network structure. Distributed processing in this mode will be marketed as a natural evolutionary step in teleprocessing with intelligent computing devices replacing remote job entry terminals, perhaps completely by the threshold of the 1980's. The market features of this approach will no doubt be mainframe computing power and security, combined with the stated wins of distributed processing for example, lower communication costs etc. IBM and other mainframe manfacturers will suggest this approach through their product line.

The second path of evolution we have labelled "distributed control". Here, the star network topology with its large central mainframe will be replaced by a distributed network topolgy with a certain parity of computing power between organizational levels in the corporation or institution. Data processing will be organizationally structured along with the network control function. Mainframes may be used in this scheme, but are not conceptually prerequisite. The distributed network topology will encourage resource sharing on a regular basis by providing an option-rich network structure of teleprocessing linkage. The marketing features of this approach will be based upon cost-performance and reliability combined with the stated wins of distributed processing. The leaders in the minicomputer industry and, perhaps, several mainframe manufacturers will support this approach.

On this chart you see an admission of doubt in the Research Program concerning the relative predominance in the 1980's of the centralized and distributed control trends of distributed processing. This doubt reflects, quite accurately we believe, an issue facing you, the users in this period. The kernel of this issue concerns itself with dynamic master/slave switching. Dynamic master/slave switching will allow for example, any two remote network nodes to inter-process without going through the corporate mainframe switchboard, for example, two regional factories exchanging assembly part requirements. The major ramifications of dynamic master/slave switching are immediate: (1) the star network topology, is discarded for a heirarchical, distributed topology, thereby changing the communications picture and (2) mixed hardware may be employed in the network architecture without tricky software emulation. The question is whether you as large ADP users will create significant market demand for this communications option, thereby urging the manufactures to comply. Your desire will ultimately determine the relative directions of these two trends. This, of course, after the decision (dare I say "inevitable") is made to go "distributed." I should add here that both trends of distributed processing lead to general purpose computing in the hierarchical data base and computer network modes. There are two roads to Rome on this issue. The question is which route is the best?